I MY BREAD MACHINE

I ♥ MY BREAD MACHINE

MORE THAN 100 RECIPES
FOR DELICIOUS HOME BAKING

ANNE SHEASBY

NOURISH
EAT WELL, LIVE WELL

First published in the UK and USA in 2017 by
Nourish, an imprint of Watkins Media Limited
19 Cecil Court
London WC2N 4EZ

enquiries@nourishbooks.com

Recipes taken from *The Breadmachine Bible*,
first published by DBP in 2009

Managing Editors: Sarah Epton and Rebecca Woods
Designer: Clare Thorpe
Commissioned photography: William Lingwood
Food Stylist: Bridget Sargeson
Prop Stylist: Helen Trent

A CIP record for this book is available from the
British Library

ISBN: 978-1-84899-317-4

10 9 8 7 6 5 4 3 2 1

Typeset in Futura

Colour reproduction by XY Digital
Printed in China

Publisher's note
While every care has been taken in compiling the
recipes for this book, Watkins Media Limited, or any
other persons who have been involved in working
on this publication, cannot accept responsibility for
any errors or omissions, inadvertent or not, that may
be found in the recipes or text, nor for any problems
that may arise as a result of preparing one of these
recipes. If you are pregnant or breastfeeding or
have any special dietary requirements or medical
conditions, it is advisable to consult a medical
professional before following any of the recipes
contained in this book.

Notes on the recipes
Unless otherwise stated:
• Use medium (US large) organic or free-range eggs
• All spoon and cup measures are level
• Do not mix metric, imperial and US cup
measurements:
    1 tsp = 5ml 1 tbsp = 15ml 1 cup = 240ml
• For all the gluten-free recipes in this book, where
applicable, we used Doves Farm (UK) gluten-free
flours. Other brands of gluten-free flours are available.
• We have included cooking temperatures for electric
and gas ovens. Remember if you have a fan-assisted
oven that you need to reduce the oven temperature
slightly (usually by around 20 degrees) and/or adjust
the cooking times. Please refer to the manufacturer's
guidelines for more specific information.
• Please note that bread machines vary, so add the
ingredients to the bread pan in the order specified
in your instruction manual (if this differs from the
instructions given in these recipes). The order in which
we recommend that you add the ingredients to your
bread pan will be applicable to many, but not all,
bread machines, so please ensure that you read and
follow your manufacturer's instruction book carefully
before preparing any of these recipes.

nourishbooks.com

CONTENTS

INTRODUCTION

BREAD OVER THE CENTURIES

Bread has been part of the staple diet of many countries worldwide for thousands of years and it is still held in high esteem within many cultures. Bread forms an important part of our everyday diet, providing a good, basic food that is both nutritious and delicious.

In centuries gone by, bread was initially baked over open fires, but gradually traditional ovens of brick or stone were built into homes or bakeries. Such ovens are still in use in the more rural areas of countries around the world, but the advance of technology and the development of modern ovens has seen the traditional types much less used. Over time, an increasing range of breads has been created, and new ingredients and flavourings have been discovered and added to basic recipes. Today we have a vast range of delicious loaves available to us in all shapes and sizes, offering many different tastes and textures.

Bakers, grocers, delicatessens, farmers' markets and supermarkets stock an array of traditional loaves as well as popular regional loaves and breads from around the world.

We can choose from sweet or savoury breads, some plain, others flavoured with ingredients such as seeds, olives, cheese, herbs, sun-dried tomatoes, spices or fruit. A wide range of organic and specialist breads, such as gluten- or dairy-free breads, is also readily available, and artisan bakers offer traditional loaves as well as creating new and interesting breads.

Nevertheless, it's hard to beat the rich aroma and full flavour of freshly made home-baked loaves, and making your own bread can be simple and very rewarding, especially with the use of a bread machine. These increasingly popular appliances are ideal for those of us with little time to spare, providing the satisfaction of baking your own bread using fresh, nourishing ingredients.

OUR DAILY BREAD

Bread is an appetizing food as well as being nutritious, and we should try to include a good proportion of starchy foods, such as bread, in our everyday diet. Many basic breads are low in fat, and bread provides an excellent source of starch – the more complex carbohydrate that provides the body with a sustained energy source – as well as some protein. All breads provide dietary fibre, and wholemeal/wholewheat and wholegrain varieties contain nearly four times more than white loaves, in addition to lots of B vitamins and some iron. White flour is often fortified with calcium, so in fact, white bread can contribute significantly to calcium intake.

Obviously, some of the more elaborate enriched breads and doughs contain more calories and fat than basic loaves, but these too can be enjoyed as special-occasion breads or treats within a balanced diet. Many of the quick breads such as teabreads can also make healthy snacks.

BREAD MACHINE RECIPES FOR ALL TYPES OF BREAD

This book by no means includes all bread machine recipes, but it offers many different types of breads from all over the world, enabling you to create tasty breads in your own home at a fraction of the cost of commercially produced loaves.

We include the basics of breadmaking and bread machines, essential information on key ingredients and techniques, as well as some useful hints and tips. Each recipe section is filled with a tempting selection of recipes, ranging from simple, rustic everyday breads to enriched, speciality loaves, and from traditional flat breads to quick and easy teabreads and tea-time treats. We also include a section on gluten-free breads, for those with a sensitivity to gluten.

Each recipe is clearly written and easy to follow, and includes guidance tips such as preparation and cooking times, as well as the number of servings.

By mastering your bread machine, and using the recipes in this book as a guide, you can experiment with all kinds of flavours, shapes and textures to suit your own tastes. So we invite you to take a leisurely journey through this eclectic collection and hope that you will enjoy the experience of creating and baking your own bread at home for many months and years to come.

BREAD BASICS

INGREDIENTS FOR BREADMAKING

Bread has four essential ingredients: flour, yeast, liquid and salt. Other ingredients such as sugar, fat and eggs may be added to produce different types of bread.

FLOUR

For traditional yeasted breads made in a bread machine, choose strong wheat flour, also known as breadmaking flour or bread flour. It is available in several varieties, the most common being white, brown, wholemeal, granary/mixed grain and soft grain white. Strong flour has a high gluten content, which stretches the dough and traps in air as it cooks, to give a well-shaped loaf with a good rise and a light, open texture. Flours vary between brands, but choose organic, unbleached strong flour, if possible.

Plain/all-purpose or self-raising/self-rising flours are generally used only in yeast-free and quick breads (although some yeasted doughs, such as French bread, use a mixture of flours). Quick breads tend to have a closer, more crumbly texture.

Breads made with strong wholemeal/ wholewheat flour tend to be slightly denser and coarser in texture than white breads, but are flavourful and nutritious. For a lighter-textured loaf, you can use half strong white and half strong wholemeal/wholewheat flour. Strong brown flour will produce a lighter brown loaf, whereas strong granary/mixed grain or malthouse flour (which is a mixture of strong brown flour and malted wheat flakes or grains), gives a nutty, malted flavour. Strong granary/mixed grain flour may also be made from a combination of strong wholemeal/wholewheat and white flours, sometimes with rye flour added, and malted wheat grains. Stoneground flour (available in wholemeal/wholewheat and brown varieties) is ground between stones, hence the name, and this gives the flour a slightly roasted, nutty flavour. Strong soft grain flour is strong white flour with kibbled grains of wheat and rye added.

Other flours such as barley, millet and spelt flours have a low gluten content, but can be combined with strong bread flours to make delicious loaves. Rye flour, which has a good gluten content, often produces dough that is sticky and difficult to handle, so it is frequently mixed with other flours to make it more manageable.

GLUTEN-FREE FLOURS

If you have an intolerance of or sensitivity to gluten, you will need to avoid flours that contain gluten. Because gluten is the protein that strengthens and binds dough in baking, you may need to find alternative binding agents when using gluten-free flours. A combination of starches often works better than a single type, and adding ingredients such as egg, grated apple or mashed banana may also help. It should be noted that gluten-free flours tend to make denser loaves with a closer texture, and also that they tend to absorb more liquid than ordinary flours, so you may need to add a little more liquid to all your dough mixtures if you are adapting standard recipes into gluten-free ones. A range of gluten-free white and bread flours is widely available from supermarkets and health food stores.

Alternatively, you can combine a selection of naturally gluten-free flours such as rice flour, gram (chickpea) flour, buckwheat flour, cornmeal or maize meal flour, tapioca flour and potato flour. Gluten-free bread mixes are also available from health food shops, and many of these are suitable for use in a bread machine.

It is important to remember when making bread by hand or using a bread machine that all utensils should be washed thoroughly before and after use, as even the slightest trace of wheat may cause an allergic reaction in someone who suffers with coeliac disease or who has an intolerance to wheat.

YEAST

Yeast is an essential ingredient in breadmaking as it causes the bread to rise. It is a living organism that feeds on the sugar and later the starches in the flour and it then releases a gas (carbon dioxide) that makes dough rise. Yeast is available in several different forms including fresh yeast, traditional or ordinary dried active yeast, and fast-action dried yeast/instant dry yeast (quick or rapid rising) or easy-blend (easy-bake) dried yeast.

For this cookbook, in all relevant recipes, we have used fast-action dried yeast/instant dry yeast (also known as easy-blend, easy-bake, quick yeast). This type of yeast is recommended for use in a bread machine and it is simple and convenient to use. Fresh yeast and traditional or ordinary dried active yeast (granules) are not suitable for use in a bread machine.

Fast-action dried yeast/instant dry yeast

Fast-action dried yeast/instant dry yeast is a combination of dried yeast and the bread improver ascorbic acid (vitamin C), which accelerates the action of the yeast during the fermentation process. It is available in handy 7g/¼oz sachets, or it can be bought in resealable foil packets or tubs of about 125g/4½oz, which need to be kept in the refrigerator once opened and used within 10–12 weeks. Yeast won't work if it is stale, so always follow instructions for storage and adhere to the use-by date on the packet.

OTHER LEAVENING INGREDIENTS

While yeast is the most common leavening ingredient used in breadmaking, other raising agents such as baking powder and bicarbonate of soda/baking soda are used for some quick breads and teabreads.

LIQUIDS

The liquid used in breadmaking is usually water, although milk or a mixture of milk and water is used in some recipes. Other liquids, such as natural yogurt or eggs, may also be used in some bread machine doughs. One main difference between making bread by hand and making bread in a bread machine is the temperature of the water or liquid used. Whereas warm water or liquid is used when making bread by hand, cold water or cool milk (at room temperature) is usually required for bread machine recipes (check your bread machine manual for specific guidance on this) – unless using the "Rapid Bake" or "Fast

Bake" programme, when warm water (or other liquid) may be required. If the timer-delay facility is being used, fresh milk should be replaced with dried skimmed milk powder and water, while eggs and other highly perishable ingredients should not be used.

SALT

Salt improves the flavour of bread and it also helps the dough to rise in a controlled and even way, resulting in a well-risen, even loaf. However, salt also slows down the action of yeast, so follow the quantities given and be careful not to add too much if you're adapting your own recipes.

SUGAR AND OTHER SWEETENERS

Sugar helps to feed the yeast and make it more active, hence encouraging fermentation to take place more quickly, but too much sugar can impede the effectiveness of yeast. Modern types of yeast, including fast-action dried yeast/instant dry yeast, no longer need sugar as the flour provides them with enough food, but for good measure it is usual to add a little sugar in bread machine recipes.

White, soft light brown and soft dark brown sugars can all be used in bread machine recipes and in some recipes honey, golden/light corn syrup, maple syrup, malt extract, black treacle or molasses are used to add flavour and colour. Artificial sweeteners are not suitable for breadmaking.

FATS

Some bread machine recipes include a little fat, such as butter or lard. Others may require the addition of oil or melted butter. Fats add flavour and richness, as well as improving the keeping qualities of the bread, but too much fat will slow down the action of the yeast. We have specified using butter in most of the recipes (where applicable), but in many cases you can use vegetable margarine or a similar alternative fat, if preferred. Low-fat spreads are not recommended for use in a bread machine.

BREAD MIXES

There is a good range of bread mixes available, many of which are suitable for use in a bread machine, and they are ideal for creating delicious home-baked breads with the minimum of fuss. They include white, wholemeal, granary/mixed grain and seed bread mixes as well as a range of flavoured varieties. Gluten-free bread mixes are also available.

Simply follow the instructions given on the packet and also refer to your manufacturer's instructions for more advice. Check that the weight of the ingredients in the packet does not exceed the total amount your bread machine can handle, and check the consistency of the dough after 5 minutes, adding a little extra liquid if the mixture seems too dry.

Bread mixes are best baked immediately rather than using a timer-delay facility, as you cannot separate the yeast from the liquid.

BREADMAKING TECHNIQUES

Please note that the following information is applicable only if you are using the "Dough" programme on your bread machine. It does not apply to loaves that are made and baked completely in a bread machine.

KNOCKING BACK AND PROVING THE DOUGH

If you are using the "Dough" programme on your bread machine, once this programme has finished, the dough is removed from the bread pan and then it is knocked back. This process will smooth out any large air pockets and ensure an even texture in the bread. To knock back the dough, turn it onto a lightly floured surface, then punch the risen dough with your fist to deflate it and knock out the air. Knead it briefly – for about 2–3 minutes – to redistribute the yeast and the gases formed by fermentation. Sometimes, at this stage, other ingredients such as olives, chopped herbs, chopped sun-dried tomatoes, chopped nuts, seeds or dried fruit may be kneaded into the dough (if they have not already been added during the "Dough" cycle).

The dough is then shaped or moulded as required, covered and left in a warm place until it has doubled in size. This is known as the proving stage. It is important not to over-prove the dough, otherwise the bread may collapse during baking – make sure the dough rises only until it is doubled in size. However, if it does not rise enough at this stage the loaf will be dense and flat. To test if the dough has risen enough, simply press it lightly with your fingertip. It should feel springy and the indentation made by your finger should slowly spring back and fill.

For professional-looking bread, proving baskets (often used by professional bakers) may be used for proving the dough. These are wicker baskets lined with linen or canvas, which are lightly floured, and they provide extra support to the bread during its final rising. They are available in round or long (baguette) shapes from good kitchenware shops. Once the dough has been proved in a basket, simply turn it out onto a baking sheet and bake as normal.

SHAPING BREAD

If you are using the "Dough" programme on your bread machine, once this programme has finished and you have knocked back the dough, it can be shaped by hand in various ways. Common shapes include cottage loaf, large round or oval, plait (or braid) and baton. Dough can be formed into rolls of varying sizes and shapes including rounds, knots, long rolls and rings. It can be slashed with a sharp knife in various ways before or after proving: slash the top of the loaf along its length; make criss-cross lines over the top; cut a deep cross over the centre, or several diagonal slashes across the top of the loaf.

Slashing the tops of loaves is done not only for visual effect but also for practical reasons, to provide escape routes for the air and to control the direction and extent of the rise during baking. The earlier you slash the dough, the wider the splits in the baked loaf; and the deeper the slashes, the more the bread will open during baking. Use a sharp knife and a swift, smooth action when slashing the dough, to avoid tearing it.

GLAZING BREAD

If you are using the "Dough" programme on your bread machine, once this programme has finished and you have knocked back and shaped the dough, brushing a loaf with a glaze before baking will enhance the colour of the bread, as well as adding flavour to the crust. Glazes not only help to give the baked bread an attractive finish, but they also add moisture to the loaf (by producing steam which helps to expand the loaf and ensure even cooking). Glazes also help toppings or garnishes that you may wish to add to loaves or rolls to stick to the surface of the dough.

Breads may be glazed before (sometimes during) or just after baking. The most common ingredients used to glaze loaves are water, milk or beaten egg, but you can also try melted butter, olive oil, single/light cream, warmed clear honey, sugar syrup or a thin glacé icing for a variety of different finishes.

FINISHING TOUCHES FOR BREAD

Once the dough has been shaped and glazed and before it is baked, various ingredients can be used for topping or finishing the bread, and each ingredient will create a different effect. Try sprinkling loaves or rolls with seeds, cracked or kibbled wheat, rolled oats, salt flakes, grated cheese or fresh herbs before baking, or dust with a little flour. For sweet breads, try dusting with icing/confectioners' sugar or sprinkling with sugar, chopped nuts, flaked/sliced almonds, dried fruits or grated chocolate, usually after baking.

Some enriched or speciality doughs may need covering to stop them browning too much during baking. If the bread begins to brown too quickly, cover it loosely with foil towards the end of the cooking time.

STORING BREAD

Most homemade bread is at its best when served freshly baked on the day it is made, and it should be eaten within 1–2 days as it stales quite quickly. Bread made from enriched doughs, with a high fat or sugar content, is also best eaten when freshly baked, but will keep longer, for up to 2–3 days.

Bread is best stored in a cool, dry, well-ventilated bread bin or an earthenware bread crock, and not in the refrigerator (the cold draws moisture out of the loaf, making it dry and stale). Wrap bread in foil or a polythene food bag if it has a soft crust, and in a paper or fabric bag if it is crusty.

Bread also freezes well for a short time – up to about 1 month. Simply seal the bread in a polythene freezer bag, or alternatively, cut the loaf in half or into slices and freeze in convenient portions, ideal for defrosting when required. Defrost frozen breads at room temperature.

Quick and yeast-free breads tend to stale quickly and these are often best eaten freshly baked or within 1–2 days. Many shop-bought breads contain preservatives or flour improvers, hence they have a longer storage life than homemade breads.

BREAD MACHINES

There is a wide range of bread machines to choose from and selecting a model to suit you will depend on several factors, including size or capacity required and budget. Do some research before buying a bread machine to ensure it is the right model to suit you.

Bread machines save time and effort and they are relatively simple to use. Before you begin, it is worth familiarizing yourself with your machine and experimenting with the different programmes and options. Make a few of the basic breads in your bread machine manual before you try any new recipes. Practice makes perfect and you will soon master how to use your machine.

The names of the programmes, such as "Rapid Bake" or "Basic White", may differ from one model to another. The delay-timer facility is useful for when you are not at home or are asleep – coming home or waking up to the smell of freshly baked bread is wonderful!

Programmes vary between models, but many include a "Basic White" or "Normal"; "Wholewheat" or "Wholemeal"; "Multigrain"; "Rapid Bake" or "Fast Bake"; "Sweet", "Raisin Bake" or "Raisin Beep"; "Dough"; "Raisin Dough"; and "Bake Only" programmes. Some models may also include more specialised programmes such as "French", "Cake", "Sandwich", "Pizza", "Jam"/ "Compote", or a Gluten-free option. Refer to your instruction manual for more details of the programmes included in your bread machine.

Some bread machines include other features like an automatic dispenser (for adding extra ingredients) or a speciality mode for different grains and flours. Some also offer a choice of three crust colours: light, medium or dark. However, if your machine does not have this option or you would prefer a darker crust once the loaf has been baked, simply brush the top of the baked loaf with melted butter, or egg yolk mixed with water, and brown under a hot grill or in a preheated oven at 200°C/400°F/gas 6 for 5–10 minutes.

Bread machine pans vary in size between models and on large models you may have the option of making up to three different sizes of loaf. We have selected a medium-sized loaf for these recipes (where relevant), which should suit most bread machines.

We have given ingredient quantities and cooking instructions for each recipe in this book, but it is very important that you read through your manufacturer's guidelines before embarking on any of the recipes. Bread machines vary, so you may find, for example, that you have to add the ingredients to the bread pan in a slightly different order from that given in a recipe. Simply add the ingredients to the bread pan in the order specified in your instruction manual.

USEFUL TIPS WHEN USING A BREAD MACHINE

- Take the bread pan out of the machine before adding the ingredients. As well as making weighing out easier, it also avoids spillage in the bread machine body.
- Accurate measuring is probably the most crucial factor for a successful loaf when using a bread machine. Always use a proper set of measuring spoons. Many models include a measuring spoon and measuring cup for liquids, so use these if they are provided.
- It is important that the salt, sugar and yeast are kept separate from each other in the bread pan until mixing commences. This

is less important if you are making some breads using the "Rapid Bake" or "Fast Bake" programme, as the ingredients are mixed as soon as the programme begins.

- Keep the yeast dry and separate from any liquids added to the bread pan until mixing commences. Separate the yeast from the liquid by adding the yeast before or after the flour (according to your instruction manual) – the flour acts as a temporary barrier between the yeast and liquid.

- Once the initial mixing cycle has begun, if you are able to, it is worth briefly lifting the lid and scraping down the sides of the bread pan using a flexible plastic or rubber spatula, to ensure even mixing, in case some of the ingredients stick to the corners of the bread pan.

- Once your bread machine is in rising or baking mode, resist the temptation to open the lid, as the cold air will interfere with the temperature inside the machine and may slow things down. Some models incorporate a viewing window so that you can check on your bread's progress.

- When using the "Raisin Bake" or "Raisin Beep" programme, add extra ingredients and flavourings when the machine makes an audible sound or beep. Check that all the ingredients have mixed in and use a flexible plastic or rubber spatula to scrape down the sides of the bread

pan, if necessary. If you do not have this facility on your machine, add the extra ingredients about 5 minutes before the end of the kneading cycle.

- If you are using the "Dough" programme, once this programme has finished and you have knocked back and shaped the dough, the shaped loaf or rolls should be placed on either a greased or a floured baking sheet(s) (or other tin/pan) before baking. Some enriched or speciality breads are best baked on a greased rather than a floured baking sheet, to avoid sticking. With each recipe, we include guidelines on preparing the bread pan, baking sheets or other tins/pans, where applicable.

- In some recipes, we use the "Bake Only" programme, which is ideal for "baking" recipes such as teabreads, tealoaves, cakes, etc. Many bread machines include this programme but some don't, so choose these recipes only if your bread machine includes this facility.

- When using the "Bake Only" programme (for example, when making teabreads or cakes), remove the kneading blade or paddle (if possible) from the bread pan before use. Grease and line the base of the bread pan with non-stick baking paper or greaseproof/wax paper before adding the teabread (or cake) mixture. With some bread machines, the kneading blade is a fixed part of the bread pan and cannot be removed.

- When using the "Bake Only" programme, remove the bread pan from the machine before transferring the teabread or cake mixture to the pan. Then place the bread pan back in position in the bread machine before closing the lid and proceeding with the baking process.

- When using the "Bake Only" programme, set the timer, if possible, to the minimum time recommended in the recipe (or according to the manufacturer's instruction manual). Check the loaf after the shortest recommended time – and before the timer has finished, if necessary – and remove the baked loaf if it is ready. With some bread machines, you can set the timer for as long as you wish (within reason), whilst on others the timer is preset to a specific amount of time – with some bread machines this preset time can be reset immediately once the initial baking time has finished (if the recipe needs further baking time, for example), whilst with other models the timer cannot be reset straight away, so bear this in mind when choosing recipes to make in your particular bread machine. Your manufacturer's guidelines should give you more advice about this.

- Even if you don't use the timer-delay facility on your bread machine, the timer itself will be invaluable when you are making bread, so that you can see how many minutes are left to run on the programme.

- Don't touch the outside of the bread machine during the baking cycle as it can sometimes get quite hot and may cause burns if you are not careful.

- Once the bread is baked, always take the bread pan out of the machine using oven gloves.

GLUTEN-FREE BREADS

When making gluten-free breads in a bread machine, it is important to refer to the manufacturer's instructions for guidance on the specific programmes recommended. The "Rapid Bake" or "Fast Bake" programme will usually produce the best results. Some bread machines include a specific Gluten-free programme/option.

BREAD MACHINE RECIPES – TROUBLE-SHOOTING

Things can occasionally go wrong when making bread in a bread machine and it is useful to know what may have gone wrong. Most, if not all, bread machines include a trouble-shooting guide which details common errors, including problems with loaf size and shape, bread texture and crust colour and thickness, as well as bread pan problems and operational errors. Please refer to your manufacturer's instruction manual for more details.

ADAPTING RECIPES FOR USE IN A BREAD MACHINE

There is no easy formula for adapting conventional recipes for the bread machine, but the best advice is to look through the recipes in this book to find one that is similar and use as a rough guide. It is also worth checking your manufacturer's instruction manual as this may give advice for adapting your own recipes to suit that particular model. Once you have tried a few recipes in your bread machine, you will soon get the feel for how to adapt your own recipes.

USEFUL TIPS FOR ADAPTING YOUR OWN RECIPES

- First make sure you use the correct quantities for the bread machine, ensuring that the total quantity of ingredients will fit into your bread pan. Do not exceed the recommended maximum. If necessary, reduce the flour and liquid quantities to match the quantities in a similar recipe.

- Use the flour and water quantities given in the recipes in this book as a guide and always refer to your manufacturer's instruction book. Keep the flour and liquid in the correct proportions. You may find that you need to add a little more water than the amount given in hand-made recipes, but this will vary depending on several factors such as the type of recipe itself, other ingredients used, etc. With a bit of practice, you will soon get the feel for approximately how much liquid to add to different basic quantities of flour.

- Always replace fresh yeast and traditional or ordinary dried active yeast (granules) with an appropriate amount of fast-action dried yeast/instant dry yeast (for more details refer to your manufacturer's guidelines). As a rough guide for wholemeal/wholewheat bread, try using 1 teaspoon fast-action dried yeast/instant dry yeast for up to 375g/13oz/2⅔ cups flour or 1½ teaspoons fast-action dried yeast/instant dry yeast for up to 675g/1½lb/4⅔ cups flour.

- If the timer-delay facility is being used, fresh milk should be replaced with dried skimmed milk powder and water, while eggs and other highly perishable ingredients should not be used.

- If your conventional recipe uses egg, include the egg as part of the total liquid measurement.

- Check the consistency of the dough during the first few minutes of mixing. Bread machines require a slightly softer dough than is needed for hand-made breads, so you may need to add a little extra liquid. The dough should be wet enough to relax back gradually. If the dough is crumbly or the machine seems to be labouring, add a little extra water. If the dough is sticking to the sides of the pan and doesn't form a ball, add a little extra flour.

BASIC & EVERYDAY BREADS

In this chapter you will find a selection of delicious breads that are ideal for regular baking. We include basic loaves, cobbs and plaits as well as a collection of slightly more unusual flavoured breads that are enjoyed all over the world, many on a daily basis.

Choose from rustic, homely bread recipes such as Garden Herb Bread, Honey Oatmeal Bread, Cottage Loaf, Milk Loaf and Flowerpot Breads. Or try authentic recipes from the rest of Europe and further afield such as French Bread, Pesto Whirl Bread or Greek Black Olive Bread, as well as Herby Polenta Bread, Caraway Seed Bread or Garlic Bubble Ring.

BASIC BROWN BREAD

PREPARATION TIME 10 minutes

COOKING TIME varies according to
    bread machine

MAKES 1 loaf (serves 10)

350ml/12fl oz/1½ cups water

250g/9oz/1¾ cups strong wholemeal/
    wholewheat flour

250g/9oz/1¾ cups strong white flour

1 tbsp skimmed milk powder

1½ tsp salt

2 tsp granulated sugar

25g/1oz/2 tbsp butter, diced

1 tsp fast-action dried yeast/instant dry yeast

Pour the water into the bread pan. Sprinkle over
each type of flour in turn, covering the water
completely. Sprinkle the milk powder over the flour.
Place the salt, sugar and butter in separate corners
of the pan. Make a small indent in the centre of
the flour and add the yeast.

Close the lid, set the machine to "Basic White"/
"Normal" or "Wholewheat" (or equivalent), then
select the loaf size and crust type. Press Start.

After baking, remove the bread pan from the
machine and turn the loaf out onto a wire rack
to cool. Serve in slices.

BASIC WHITE BREAD

PREPARATION TIME 10 minutes

COOKING TIME varies according to
    bread machine

MAKES 1 loaf (serves 10)

350ml/12fl oz/1½ cups water

500g/1lb 2oz/3½ cups strong white flour

1 tbsp skimmed milk powder

1½ tsp salt

2 tsp granulated sugar

25g/1oz/2 tbsp butter, diced

1 tsp fast-action dried yeast/instant dry yeast

Pour the water into the bread pan. Sprinkle over
the flour, covering the water completely. Sprinkle
the milk powder over the flour. Place the salt,
sugar and butter in separate corners of the pan.
Make a small indent in the centre of the flour and
add the yeast.

Close the lid, set the machine to "Basic White"/
"Normal" (or equivalent), then select the loaf size
and crust type. Press Start.

After baking, remove the bread pan from the
machine and turn the loaf out onto a wire rack
to cool. Serve in slices.

COTTAGE LOAF

PREPARATION TIME 20 minutes, plus mixing & kneading time in bread machine, plus rising & resting

COOKING TIME 30–35 minutes

MAKES 1 loaf (serves 10–12)

325ml/11fl oz /1⅓ cups warm water
(or according to bread mix packet instructions)
500g/1lb 2oz packet white bread mix
1 tsp salt
strong white flour, for dusting

Pour the water into the bread pan. (For a good-shaped cottage loaf, the dough needs to be firm enough for the bottom round to support the top piece without sagging, so you may not need to add all the water.) Sprinkle over the bread mix, covering the water completely. Close the lid, set the machine to "Dough" and press Start.

Meanwhile, grease or flour two baking sheets and set aside. When the dough is ready, remove it from the machine, knock it back on a lightly floured surface, then cut off one third of the dough. Shape each portion into plump balls and place each one on a baking sheet. Cover and leave to rise in a warm place until doubled in size.

Preheat the oven to 220°C/425°F/gas 7. Gently flatten the balls of dough and carefully place the smaller ball on top of the larger one. Gently push the floured handle of a wooden spoon down through the centre of the dough to join the two pieces together, then slightly enlarge the hole with your fingers. Leave to rest for 5–10 minutes.

Dissolve the salt in 1 tablespoon of hot water, then lightly brush over the loaf and dust with a little flour. Using a sharp knife, make slashes around the top and base of the bread.

Bake for about 30–35 minutes, or until the bread is golden brown and sounds hollow when tapped underneath. Transfer to a wire rack to cool.

FARMHOUSE LOAF

PREPARATION TIME 10 minutes

COOKING TIME varies according to
 bread machine

MAKES 1 loaf (serves 10)

350ml/12fl oz/1½ cups water

400g/14oz/3 cups strong white flour, plus extra
 for dusting

115g/4oz/¾ cup plus 1 tbsp strong wholemeal/
 wholewheat flour

1 tbsp skimmed milk powder

1½ tsp salt

2 tsp light soft brown sugar

25g/1oz/2 tbsp butter, diced

1½ tsp fast-action dried yeast/instant dry yeast

Pour the water into the bread pan. Sprinkle over
each type of flour in turn, covering the water
completely. Sprinkle the milk powder over the flour.
Place the salt, sugar and butter in separate corners
of the pan. Make a small indent in the centre of
the flour and add the yeast.

Close the lid, set the machine to "Basic White"/
"Normal" (or equivalent), then select the loaf size
and crust type. Press Start. If possible, 10 minutes
before the baking cycle starts, brush the top of the
loaf with water and dust with a little flour. Using
a sharp knife, cut a slash, about 1cm/½in deep,
along the length of the loaf.

After baking, remove the bread pan from the
machine and turn the loaf out onto a wire rack
to cool. Serve in slices.

HOME-STYLE WHOLEMEAL BREAD

PREPARATION TIME 10 minutes

COOKING TIME varies according to
 bread machine

MAKES 1 loaf (serves 10)

350ml/12fl oz/1½ cups water

400g/14oz/3 cups strong wholemeal/
 wholewheat flour

115g/4oz/¾ cup plus 1 tbsp strong white flour

1½ tsp salt

2 tsp granulated sugar

25g/1oz/2 tbsp butter, diced

1 tsp fast-action dried yeast/instant dry yeast

Pour the water into the bread pan. Sprinkle over
each type of flour in turn, covering the water
completely. Place the salt, sugar and butter in
separate corners of the pan. Make a small indent
in the centre of the flour and add the yeast.

Close the lid, set the machine to "Wholewheat"
or "Multigrain" (or equivalent), then select the loaf
size and crust type. Press Start.

After baking, remove the bread pan from the
machine and turn the loaf out onto a wire rack
to cool. Serve in slices.

HONEY OATMEAL BREAD

PREPARATION TIME 15 minutes, plus mixing & kneading time in bread machine, plus rising

COOKING TIME 30–35 minutes

MAKES 1 loaf (serves 12–14)

250ml/9fl oz/1 cup water

100ml/3½fl oz/scant ½ cup milk (at room temperature), plus extra for glazing

2 tbsp thick (set) honey

450g/1lb/3¼ cups strong brown flour

115g/4oz/1 heaped cup rolled oats, plus extra for sprinkling

1½ tsp salt

1 tsp granulated sugar

25g/1oz/2 tbsp butter, diced

1½ tsp fast-action dried yeast/instant dry yeast

Pour the water and milk into the bread pan, then add the honey. Sprinkle over the flour, covering the liquid completely. Sprinkle over the oats. Place the salt, sugar and butter in separate corners of the pan. Make a small indent in the centre and add the yeast. Close the lid, set the machine to "Dough" and press Start.

Grease or flour a baking sheet and set aside. When the dough is ready, remove it from the machine, knock it back on a lightly floured surface, then shape it into a round. Place on the baking sheet, cover and leave to rise in a warm place until doubled in size.

Preheat the oven to 230°C/450°F/gas 8. Slash the top of the loaf down the centre, brush with milk and sprinkle with oats.

Bake for 10 minutes, then reduce the oven temperature to 200°C/400°F/gas 6 and bake for a further 20–25 minutes, or until the bread is risen, lightly browned and sounds hollow when tapped underneath. Transfer to a wire rack to cool. Serve in slices.

MALTED WHOLEGRAIN COBB

PREPARATION TIME 15 minutes, plus mixing & kneading time in bread machine, plus rising

COOKING TIME 30–35 minutes

MAKES 1 loaf (serves 14–16)

235ml/8½fl oz/1 cup water

100ml/3½fl oz/scant ½ cup milk (at room temperature), plus extra for glazing

2 tbsp malt extract

250g/9oz/1¾ cups strong granary/ mixed grain flour

250g/9oz/1¾ cups strong wholemeal/ wholewheat flour

1½ tsp salt

2 tsp granulated sugar

25g/1oz/2 tbsp butter, diced

1½ tsp fast-action dried yeast/instant dry yeast

kibbled or cracked wheat, for sprinkling

Pour the water and milk into the bread pan, then add the malt extract. Sprinkle over each type of flour in turn, covering the liquid completely. Place the salt, sugar and butter in separate corners of the pan. Make a small indent in the centre of the flour and add the yeast. Close the lid, set the machine to "Dough" and press Start.

Grease or flour a baking sheet and set aside. When the dough is ready, remove it from the machine, knock it back on a lightly floured surface, then shape it into a large round. Place on the baking sheet, cover and leave to rise in a warm place until doubled in size.

Preheat the oven to 230°C/450°F/gas 8. Cut a cross shape into the top of the loaf, brush with a little milk and sprinkle with kibbled or cracked wheat.

Bake for 10 minutes, then reduce the oven temperature to 200°C/400°F/gas 6 and bake for a further 20–25 minutes, or until the bread is risen, lightly browned and sounds hollow when tapped underneath. Transfer to a wire rack to cool. Serve in slices.

FRENCH BREAD

PREPARATION TIME 15 minutes, plus mixing & kneading time in bread machine, plus rising
COOKING TIME 15–20 minutes
MAKES 2 French sticks (each loaf serves 4–6)

300ml/10½ fl oz/1¼ cups water
400g/14oz/3 cups strong white flour
55g/2oz/⅓ cup plus 1 tbsp plain/all-purpose white flour
1½ tsp salt
1 tsp granulated sugar
1 tsp fast-action dried yeast/instant dry yeast

Pour the water into the bread pan. Sprinkle over each type of flour in turn, covering the water completely. Place the salt and sugar in separate corners of the pan. Make a small indent in the centre of the flour and add the yeast. Close the lid, set the machine to "French Dough" (or equivalent) and press Start.

Meanwhile, flour a large baking sheet and set aside. When the dough is ready, remove it from the machine and knock it back on a lightly floured surface. Divide the dough in half and roll out each portion to make a rectangle about 20 x 7.5cm/ 8 x 3in. Starting from a long edge, carefully roll up each rectangle of dough like a Swiss roll.

Gently roll and stretch each piece of dough to make a loaf about 28–33cm/11–13in long. Place between the folds of a pleated tea towel for support, cover and leave to rise in a warm place until doubled in size.

Preheat the oven to 220°C/425°F/gas 7. Roll the loaves onto the baking sheet. Using a sharp knife, cut several diagonal slashes in the top of each loaf at regular intervals. Spray the inside of the hot oven with water, then immediately bake the loaves for 15–20 minutes, or until crisp and golden brown. Transfer to a wire rack to cool. Serve warm or cold.

CARAWAY CHEESE LOAF

PREPARATION TIME 15 minutes, plus mixing & kneading time in bread machine, plus rising

COOKING TIME 30 minutes

· MAKES 1 loaf (serves 10–12)

300ml/10½ fl oz/1¼ cups milk (at room temperature), plus extra for glazing

450g/1lb/3¼ cups strong white flour

2 tsp mustard powder

1 tbsp caraway seeds

25g/1oz/2 tbsp freshly grated Parmesan cheese

115g/4oz/1 cup finely grated mature/sharp Cheddar cheese

1¼ tsp salt

1½ tsp caster/superfine sugar

1½ tsp fast-action dried yeast/instant dry yeast

Pour the milk into the bread pan. Sprinkle over the flour, covering the milk completely, then sprinkle over the mustard powder, 2 teaspoons of the caraway seeds, the Parmesan cheese and 85g/3oz/⅔ cup of the Cheddar cheese. Place the salt and sugar in separate corners of the pan. Make a small indent in the centre of the flour and add the yeast. Close the lid, set the machine to "Dough" and press Start.

Meanwhile, grease or flour a baking sheet and set aside. When the dough is ready, remove it from the machine and knock it back on a lightly floured surface, then shape the dough into a 15cm (6in) round and place on the baking sheet. Cover and leave to rise in a warm place until doubled in size.

Preheat the oven to 230°C/450°F/gas 8. Using a sharp knife, cut a shallow cross in the top of the loaf, then brush with a little milk. Mix together the remaining caraway seeds and Cheddar cheese and sprinkle over the top of the loaf.

Bake the loaf for 10 minutes, then reduce the oven temperature to 200°C/400°F/gas 6 and bake for a further 20 minutes, or until the bread is risen, golden brown and sounds hollow when tapped underneath. Cover the loaf loosely with foil halfway through the cooking time if it is browning too much. Transfer to a wire rack to cool. Serve in slices.

CARAWAY SEED BREAD

PREPARATION TIME 10 minutes

COOKING TIME varies according to bread machine

MAKES 1 loaf (serves 10)

350ml/12fl oz/1½ cups water

2 tbsp clear honey

400g/14oz/3 cups strong wholemeal/
wholewheat flour

115g/4oz/¾ cup plus 1 tbsp strong white flour

2 tbsp caraway seeds

2 tbsp skimmed milk powder

1½ tsp salt

25g/1oz/2 tbsp butter, diced

1 tsp fast-action dried yeast/instant dry yeast

Pour the water into the bread pan, then add the honey. Sprinkle over each type of flour in turn, covering the liquid completely. Sprinkle the caraway seeds over the flour, then sprinkle the milk powder over the seeds. Place the salt and butter in separate corners of the pan. Make a small indent in the centre of the flour and add the yeast.

Close the lid, set the machine to "Multigrain" or "Wholewheat" (or equivalent), then select the loaf size and crust type. Press Start.

After baking, remove the bread pan from the machine and turn the loaf out onto a wire rack to cool. Serve in slices.

VARIATIONS Use cumin or fennel seeds in place of the caraway seeds. Use maple syrup in place of the honey.

SEEDED RYE BREAD

PREPARATION TIME 10 minutes

COOKING TIME varies according to
   bread machine

MAKES 1 loaf (serves 10)

350ml/12fl oz/1½ cups water

1 tbsp clear honey

400g/14oz/3 cups strong white flour

115g/4oz/¾ cup plus 1 tbsp rye flour

2 tbsp caraway seeds

2 tbsp skimmed milk powder

1½ tsp salt

25g/1oz/2 tbsp butter, diced

1 tsp fast-action dried yeast/instant dry yeast

Pour the water into the bread pan, then add
the honey. Sprinkle over each type of flour in
turn, covering the liquid completely. Sprinkle the
caraway seeds over the flour, then sprinkle the
milk powder over the seeds. Place the salt and
butter in separate corners of the pan. Make a
small indent in the centre of the flour and add
the yeast.

Close the lid, set the machine to "Basic White"/
"Normal" (or equivalent), then select the loaf size
and crust type. Press Start.

After baking, remove the bread pan from the
machine and turn the loaf out onto a wire rack
to cool. Serve in slices.

SUNFLOWER SEED LOAF

PREPARATION TIME 10 minutes

COOKING TIME varies according to
   bread machine

MAKES 1 loaf (serves 10)

300ml/10½ fl oz/1¼ cups water

2 tbsp sunflower oil

225g/8oz/1⅔ cups strong white flour

225g/8oz/1⅔ cups strong granary/mixed
   grain flour

1 tbsp skimmed milk powder

1½ tsp salt

2 tsp granulated sugar

1 tsp fast-action dried yeast/instant dry yeast

5 tbsp sunflower seeds

Pour the water into the bread pan, then add
the oil. Sprinkle over each type of flour in turn,
covering the liquid completely. Sprinkle the milk
powder over the flour. Place the salt and sugar in
separate corners of the pan. Make a small indent
in the centre of the flour and add the yeast.

Close the lid, set the machine to "Basic White"/
"Normal", with "Raisin", if available (or equivalent),
then select the loaf size and crust type. Press Start.

Add the sunflower seeds when the machine makes
a sound (beeps) to add extra ingredients during
the kneading cycle (or add 5 minutes before the
end of the kneading cycle).

After baking, remove the bread pan from the
machine and turn the loaf out onto a wire rack
to cool. Serve in slices.

SIX-SEED BREAD

PREPARATION TIME 10 minutes

COOKING TIME varies according to bread machine

MAKES 1 loaf (serves 10)

300ml/10½ fl oz/1¼ cups water

2 tbsp sunflower oil

225g/8oz/1⅔ cups strong white flour

225g/8oz/1⅔ cups strong granary/mixed grain flour

1 tbsp skimmed milk powder

1½ tsp salt

2 tsp granulated sugar

1 tsp fast-action dried yeast/instant dry yeast

2 tbsp sunflower seeds

1 tbsp pumpkin seeds

2 tsp sesame seeds

2 tsp poppy seeds

1 tsp caraway seeds

1 tsp cumin or fennel seeds

Pour the water into the bread pan, then add the oil. Sprinkle over each type of flour in turn, covering the liquid completely. Sprinkle the milk powder over the flour. Place the salt and sugar in separate corners of the pan. Make a small indent in the centre of the flour and add the yeast.

Close the lid, set the machine to "Basic White"/ "Normal", with "Raisin", if available (or equivalent), then select the loaf size and crust type. Press Start.

Combine the seeds. Add the mixed seeds when the machine makes a sound (beeps) to add extra ingredients during the kneading cycle (or add 5 minutes before the end of the kneading cycle).

After baking, remove the bread pan from the machine and turn the loaf out onto a wire rack to cool. Serve in slices.

VARIATION Packets of prepared mixed seeds suitable for bread-making are available. Use 5 tablespoons of ready-mixed seeds in place of the seeds listed above.

CHEESE & SESAME SEED COBB

PREPARATION TIME 15 minutes, plus mixing & kneading time in bread machine, plus rising

COOKING TIME 35–45 minutes

MAKES 1 loaf (serves 10)

300ml/10½ fl oz/1¼ cups milk (at room temperature), plus extra for glazing

450g/1lb/3¼ cups strong white flour

2 tsp mustard powder

a few turns of freshly ground black pepper

85g/3oz/⅔ cup finely grated Gruyère or Emmental cheese

1¼ tsp salt

1½ tsp caster/superfine sugar

25g/1oz/2 tbsp butter, diced

1½ tsp fast-action dried yeast/instant dry yeast

sesame seeds, for sprinkling

Pour the milk into the bread pan. Sprinkle over the flour, covering the milk completely, then sprinkle over the mustard powder, black pepper and cheese. Place the salt, sugar and butter in separate corners of the pan. Make a small indent in the centre of the flour and add the yeast. Close the lid, set the machine to "Dough" and press Start.

Meanwhile, grease or flour a baking sheet and set aside. When the dough is ready, remove it from the machine and knock it back on a lightly floured surface, then shape the dough into a round cobb and place on the baking sheet. Cover and leave to rise in a warm place until doubled in size.

Preheat the oven to 190°C/375°F/gas 5. Lightly brush the top of the loaf with milk and sprinkle with sesame seeds.

Bake for 35–45 minutes, or until the bread is risen, golden brown and sounds hollow when tapped underneath. Transfer to a wire rack to cool. Serve in slices.

GARDEN HERB BREAD

PREPARATION TIME 10 minutes

COOKING TIME varies according to bread machine

MAKES 1 loaf (serves 10)

350ml/12fl oz/1½ cups water

500g/1lb 2oz/3½ cups strong white flour

1 tbsp skimmed milk powder

2 tbsp chopped fresh parsley

2 tbsp chopped fresh chives

2 tsp chopped fresh thyme

1½ tsp salt

2 tsp granulated sugar

25g/1oz/2 tbsp butter, diced

1 tsp fast-action dried yeast/instant dry yeast

Pour the water into the bread pan. Sprinkle over the flour, covering the water completely. Sprinkle the milk powder over the flour. Combine the herbs, then sprinkle them over the milk powder. Place the salt, sugar and butter in separate corners of the pan. Make a small indent in the centre of the flour and add the yeast.

Close the lid, set the machine to "Basic White"/ "Normal" (or equivalent), then select the loaf size and crust type. Press Start.

After baking, remove the bread pan from the machine and turn the loaf out onto a wire rack to cool. Serve in slices.

VARIATION Use 2 tablespoons of chopped fresh coriander/cilantro or basil in place of the thyme.

GRANARY HERB LOAF

PREPARATION TIME 10 minutes

COOKING TIME varies according to
 bread machine

MAKES 1 loaf (serves 10)

300ml/10½ fl oz/1¼ cups water

450g/1lb/3¼ cups strong malted
 granary/mixed grain flour

1 tbsp skimmed milk powder

1 tbsp chopped fresh mixed herbs,
 such as chives, sage and marjoram

1 tbsp chopped fresh parsley

1½ tsp freshly ground black pepper

2 tsp salt

2 tsp caster/superfine sugar

25g/1oz/2 tbsp butter, diced

1½ tsp fast-action dried yeast/instant dry yeast

Pour the water into the bread pan. Sprinkle over the flour, covering the water completely. Sprinkle the milk powder over the flour. Combine the herbs and black pepper, then sprinkle these over the milk powder. Place the salt, sugar and butter in separate corners of the pan. Make a small indent in the centre of the flour and add the yeast.

Close the lid, set the machine to "Wholewheat" (or equivalent), then select the loaf size and crust type. Press Start.

After baking, remove the bread pan from the machine and turn the loaf out onto a wire rack to cool. Serve in slices.

MALTED WHEAT BREAD

PREPARATION TIME 10 minutes

COOKING TIME varies according to
 bread machine

MAKES 1 loaf (serves 10)

300ml/10½ fl oz/1¼ cups water

2 tbsp malt extract

450g/1lb/3¼ cups strong granary/mixed
 grain flour

1 tbsp skimmed milk powder

1½ tsp salt

2 tsp granulated sugar

25g/1oz/2 tbsp butter, diced

1 tsp fast-action dried yeast/instant dry yeast

Pour the water into the bread pan, then add the malt extract. Sprinkle over the flour, covering the liquid completely. Sprinkle the milk powder over the flour. Place the salt, sugar and butter in separate corners of the pan. Make a small indent in the centre of the flour and add the yeast.

Close the lid, set the machine to "Wholewheat" or "Multigrain" (or equivalent), then select the loaf size and crust type. Press Start.

After baking, remove the bread pan from the machine and turn the loaf out onto a wire rack to cool. Serve in slices.

FLOWERPOT BREADS

PREPARATION TIME 15 minutes, plus mixing & kneading time in bread machine, plus rising

COOKING TIME 30–40 minutes, plus terracotta pot preparation

MAKES 2 loaves (each loaf serves 4)

315ml/10½fl oz/1¼ cups water

1 tbsp malt extract

450g/1lb/3¼ cups strong brown flour

55g/2oz/⅓ cup barley flakes,
    plus extra for sprinkling

1–2 tbsp chopped fresh mixed herbs

1½ tsp salt

2 tsp caster/superfine sugar

25g/1oz/2 tbsp butter, diced

2 tsp fast-action dried yeast/instant dry yeast

milk, for glazing

Liberally brush two new terracotta flowerpots (about 14cm/5½in in diameter and 12cm/4½in high) with vegetable oil, inside and out, then bake in a hot oven (200°C/400°F/gas 6) for about 30 minutes. Leave to cool, then repeat this process until the pots are impregnated with oil. Do not wash after use: wipe clean with paper towels. Lightly grease the pots and set aside.

Pour the water into the bread pan and add the malt extract. Sprinkle over the flour, covering the liquid completely, then sprinkle over the barley flakes and herbs. Place the salt, sugar and butter in separate corners of the pan. Make a small indent in the centre of the flour and add the yeast. Close the lid, set the machine to "Dough" and press Start.

When the dough is ready, remove it from the machine, knock it back on a lightly floured surface and divide in half. Shape and fit each piece of dough into a flowerpot – the dough should roughly half-fill the pot.

Cover and leave to rise in a warm place for 45–60 minutes, or until the dough almost reaches the top of the flowerpots.

Preheat the oven to 200°C/400°F/gas 6. Brush the loaf tops with a little milk and sprinkle with barley flakes. Bake for about 30–40 minutes, or until the bread is risen and sounds hollow when turned out and tapped underneath. Transfer to a wire rack to cool. Serve in slices.

MILK LOAF

PREPARATION TIME 10 minutes

COOKING TIME varies according to bread machine

MAKES 1 loaf (serves 10)

200ml/7fl oz/scant 1 cup milk
(at room temperature)
100ml/3½fl oz/scant ½ cup water
450g/1lb/3¼ cups strong white flour
1½ tsp salt
2 tsp granulated sugar
25g/1oz/2 tbsp butter, diced
1 tsp fast-action dried yeast/instant dry yeast

Pour the milk and water into the bread pan. Sprinkle over the flour, covering the liquid completely. Place the salt, sugar and butter in separate corners of the pan. Make a small indent in the centre of the flour and add the yeast.

Close the lid, set the machine to "Basic White"/ "Normal" (or equivalent), then select the loaf size and crust type. Press Start.

After baking, remove the bread pan from the machine and turn the loaf out onto a wire rack to cool. Serve in slices.

SUN-DRIED TOMATO BREAD

PREPARATION TIME 10 minutes

COOKING TIME varies according to
    bread machine

MAKES 1 loaf (serves 8–10)

300ml/10½ fl oz/1¼ cups water

1 tbsp oil from a jar of sun-dried tomatoes

450g/1lb/3¼ cups strong white flour

55g/2oz/⅓ cup freshly grated Parmesan cheese

1½ tsp salt

2 tsp caster/superfine sugar

1 tsp fast-action dried yeast/instant dry yeast

55g/2oz/½ cup sun-dried tomatoes in oil
    (drained weight), patted dry and chopped

Pour the water into the bread pan, then add the
oil. Sprinkle over the flour, covering the liquid
completely. Sprinkle over the Parmesan cheese.
Place the salt and sugar in separate corners of
the pan. Make a small indent in the centre of the
flour and add the yeast.

Close the lid, set the machine to "Basic White"/
"Normal", with "Raisin", if available (or equivalent),
then select the loaf size and crust type. Press Start.

Add the sun-dried tomatoes when the machine
makes a sound (beeps) to add extra ingredients
during the kneading cycle (or add 5 minutes
before the end of the kneading cycle).

After baking, remove the bread pan from the machine
and turn the loaf out onto a wire rack to cool.

BARLEY BREAD

PREPARATION TIME 15 minutes, plus mixing &
    kneading time in bread machine, plus rising

COOKING TIME 30–35 minutes

MAKES 1 loaf (serves 10–12)

350ml/12fl oz/1½ cups water

400g/14oz/3 cups strong brown flour

115g/4oz/¾ cup plus 1 tbsp barley flour

2 tsp salt

2 tsp caster/superfine sugar

1½ tsp fast-action dried yeast/instant dry yeast

Pour the water into the bread pan. Sprinkle over
each type of flour in turn, covering the water
completely. Place the salt and sugar in separate
corners of the pan. Make a small indent in the
centre of the flour and add the yeast. Close the
lid, set the machine to "Dough" and press Start.

Meanwhile, grease a 900g/2lb loaf tin and set
aside. When the dough is ready, remove it from
the machine, knock it back on a lightly floured
surface, then shape the dough into an oblong.
Place in the loaf tin, cover and leave to rise in a
warm place until doubled in size.

Preheat the oven to 230°C/450°F/gas 8. Bake
for 10 minutes, then reduce the oven temperature
to 200°C/400°F/gas 6 and bake for a further
20–25 minutes, or until the bread is risen, lightly
browned and sounds hollow when turned out and
tapped underneath. Cool on a wire rack. Serve
in slices.

HERB FLUTES

PREPARATION TIME 15 minutes, plus mixing & kneading time in bread machine, plus rising

COOKING TIME 25 minutes

MAKES 2 loaves (each loaf serves 4–6)

275ml/9½fl oz/1 cup plus 2 tbsp water

2 tbsp olive oil

450g/1lb/3¼ cups strong white flour, plus extra for dusting

1 tbsp dried herbes de Provence

55g/2oz/⅓ cup freshly grated Parmesan cheese

1¼ tsp salt

1½ tsp caster/superfine sugar

1½ tsp fast-action dried yeast/instant dry yeast

Pour the water into the bread pan, then add the oil. Sprinkle over the flour, covering the liquid completely, then sprinkle over the dried herbs and cheese. Place the salt and sugar in separate corners of the pan. Make a small indent in the centre of the flour and add the yeast. Close the lid, set the machine to "Dough" and press Start.

Meanwhile, grease or flour a large baking sheet and set aside. When the dough is ready, remove it from the machine, knock it back on a lightly floured surface, then divide it in half and shape each half into a baton about 30cm/12in long. Place on the baking sheet, cover and leave to rise in a warm place for about 45 minutes, or until doubled in size.

Preheat the oven to 220°C/425°F/gas 7. Dust each loaf with a little flour, then, using a sharp knife, slash across the top of each loaf four times diagonally at regular intervals.

Bake for about 25 minutes, or until the bread is risen, golden brown and sounds hollow when tapped underneath. Transfer to a wire rack to cool. Serve warm or cold.

PESTO WHIRL BREAD

PREPARATION TIME 20 minutes, plus mixing & kneading time in bread machine, plus rising
COOKING TIME 25–30 minutes
MAKES 1 loaf (serves 10–12)

325ml/11fl oz/1⅓ cups water
2 tbsp olive oil
500g/1lb 2oz/3½ cups strong white flour
1 tsp salt
1 tsp caster/superfine sugar
1 tsp fast-action dried yeast/instant dry yeast
4 tbsp ready-made green pesto sauce

Pour the water into the bread pan, then add the oil. Sprinkle over the flour, covering the liquid completely. Place the salt and sugar in separate corners of the pan. Make a small indent in the centre of the flour and add the yeast. Close the lid, set the machine to "Dough" and press Start.

Meanwhile, grease a 900g/2lb loaf tin and set aside. When the dough is ready, remove it from the machine, knock it back on a lightly floured surface, then roll or pat out to form a rectangle measuring about 30 x 20cm/12 x 8in.

Spread the pesto evenly over the rectangle of dough, then roll up the dough fairly tightly like a Swiss roll, starting from a short side. Re-shape slightly if necessary and place in the loaf tin. Cover and leave to rise in a warm place for about 30–45 minutes, or until doubled in size.

Preheat the oven to 220°C/425°F/gas 7. Bake for 25–30 minutes, or until the loaf is risen and golden. Turn out and cool on a wire rack. Serve in slices on its own or spread with butter.

VARIATION Use ready-made red pesto sauce in place of the traditional green pesto sauce.

Pictured on page 18

GREEK BLACK OLIVE BREAD

PREPARATION TIME 20 minutes, plus mixing & kneading time in bread machine, plus rising
COOKING TIME 30–35 minutes
MAKES 1 Loaf (serves 10–12)

325ml/11fl oz/1⅓ cups water

2 tbsp extra virgin olive oil

500g/1lb 2oz/3½ cups strong white flour,
    plus extra for dusting

1 tsp salt

1 tsp granulated sugar

1 tsp fast-action dried yeast/instant dry yeast

115g/4oz/¾ cup pitted black olives
    (drained weight), chopped

Pour the water into the bread pan, then add the oil. Sprinkle over the flour, covering the liquid completely. Place the salt and sugar in separate corners of the pan. Make a small indent in the centre of the flour and add the yeast. Close the lid, set the machine to "Dough" and press Start.

Meanwhile, grease or flour a baking sheet and set aside. When the dough is ready, remove it from the machine, knock it back on a lightly floured surface, then knead in about half of the chopped olives. Roll out to form a rectangle measuring about 35 x 25cm/14 x 10in.

Sprinkle the surface of the dough evenly with the remaining olives, then roll up fairly tightly like a Swiss roll, starting from a short side. Pinch the edges of each end together to seal. Place the loaf, seam-side down, on the baking sheet. Cover and leave to rise in a warm place until doubled in size.

Preheat the oven to 220°C/425°F/gas 7. Dust the loaf with a little sifted flour. Bake for 10 minutes, then reduce the oven temperature to 190°C/375°F/gas 5 and bake for a further 20–25 minutes, or until the bread is risen, golden brown and sounds hollow when tapped underneath. Transfer to a wire rack to cool. Serve warm or cold in slices.

PLAITED HERB BREAD

PREPARATION TIME 20 minutes, plus mixing & kneading time in bread machine, plus rising

COOKING TIME 35–45 minutes

MAKES 1 loaf (serves 10)

150ml/5fl oz/⅔ cup water

150ml/5fl oz/⅔ cup milk (at room temperature), plus extra for glazing

450g/1lb/3¼ cups strong white flour

1 tbsp dried herbes de Provence

85g/3oz/⅔ cup finely grated mature/sharp Cheddar or red Leicester cheese

1¼ tsp salt

1½ tsp caster/superfine sugar

25g/1oz/2 tbsp butter, diced

1½ tsp fast-action dried yeast/instant dry yeast

Pour the water and milk into the bread pan. Sprinkle over the flour, covering the liquid completely, then sprinkle over the dried herbs and cheese. Place the salt, sugar and butter in separate corners of the pan. Make a small indent in the centre of the flour and add the yeast. Close the lid, set the machine to "Dough" and press Start.

Meanwhile, grease or flour a baking sheet and set aside. When the dough is ready, remove it from the machine, knock it back on a lightly floured surface, then divide it in half. Roll each piece of dough into a long sausage or rope shape. Place them side by side and pinch together at one end to seal.

Loosely plait the ropes of dough together, then pinch them together at the other end. Place the plait on the baking sheet. Cover and leave to rise in a warm place until doubled in size.

Preheat the oven to 190°C/375°F/gas 5. Lightly brush the plait with milk. Bake for 35–45 minutes, or until the bread is risen, golden brown and sounds hollow when tapped underneath. Transfer to a wire rack to cool. Serve in slices.

CHEESE & POPPYSEED PLAIT

PREPARATION TIME 15 minutes, plus mixing & kneading time in bread machine, plus rising
COOKING TIME 30–40 minutes
MAKES 1 loaf (serves 10)

300ml/10½ fl oz/1¼ cups milk (at room temperature), plus extra for glazing

450g/1lb/3¼ cups strong white flour

2 tsp mustard powder

a few turns of freshly ground black pepper

85g/3oz/⅔ cup finely grated mature/sharp Cheddar cheese

1¼ tsp salt

1½ tsp caster/superfine sugar

25g/1oz/2 tbsp butter, diced

1½ tsp fast-action dried yeast/instant dry yeast

poppy seeds, for sprinkling

Pour the milk into the bread pan. Sprinkle over the flour, covering the milk completely, then sprinkle over the mustard powder, black pepper and cheese. Place the salt, sugar and butter in separate corners of the pan. Make a small indent in the centre of the flour and add the yeast.

Close the lid, set the machine to "Dough" and press Start.

Meanwhile, grease or flour a baking sheet and set aside. When the dough is ready, remove it from the machine, knock it back on a lightly floured surface, then divide it in half. Roll each piece of dough into a long sausage or rope shape. Pinch them together at one end to seal.

Loosely plait the ropes of dough together, then pinch them together at the other end. Place the plait on the baking sheet. Cover and leave to rise in a warm place until doubled in size.

Preheat the oven to 190°C/375°F/gas 5. Brush the plait with a little milk and sprinkle with poppy seeds.

Bake for 30–40 minutes, or until the bread is risen, golden brown and sounds hollow when tapped underneath. Transfer to a wire rack to cool. Serve in slices.

CHEESE & GRAIN COBB

PREPARATION TIME 15 minutes, plus mixing & kneading time in bread machine, plus rising

COOKING TIME 35–45 minutes

MAKES 1 loaf (serves 10–12)

300ml/10½ fl oz/1¼ cups milk (at room temperature), plus extra for glazing

450g/1lb/3¼ cups strong granary/ mixed grain flour

2 tsp mustard powder

a few turns of freshly ground black pepper

85g/3oz/⅔ cup finely grated red Leicester or mature/sharp Cheddar cheese

1½ tsp salt

1½ tsp granulated sugar

25g/1oz/2 tbsp butter, diced

1½ tsp fast-action dried yeast/instant dry yeast

kibbled or cracked wheat, for sprinkling

Pour the milk into the bread pan. Sprinkle over the flour, covering the milk completely, then sprinkle over the mustard powder, black pepper and cheese. Place the salt, sugar and butter in separate corners of the pan. Make a small indent in the centre of the flour and add the yeast. Close the lid, set the machine to "Dough" and press Start.

Meanwhile, grease or flour a baking sheet and set aside. When the dough is ready, remove it from the machine and knock it back on a lightly floured surface, then shape the dough into a round cobb and place on the baking sheet. Cover and leave to rise in a warm place for 30–45 minutes, or until doubled in size.

Preheat the oven to 190°C/375°F/gas 5. Lightly brush the top of the loaf with milk, then sprinkle with kibbled or cracked wheat.

Bake for 35–45 minutes, or until the bread is risen, golden brown and sounds hollow when tapped underneath. Transfer to a wire rack to cool. Serve in slices.

GARLIC BUBBLE RING

PREPARATION TIME 20 minutes, plus mixing & kneading time in bread machine, plus rising
COOKING TIME 30–40 minutes
MAKES 1 loaf (serves 12)

325ml/11fl oz/1⅓ cups warm water
(or according to bread mix packet instructions)
500g/1lb 2oz packet white bread mix
100g/3½oz/7 tbsp butter, melted
1 egg, beaten
25g/1oz/2 tbsp freshly grated Parmesan cheese
2 garlic cloves, crushed
½ tsp salt
1 tsp dried Italian herb seasoning

Pour the correct amount of water into the bread pan. Sprinkle over the bread mix, covering the water completely. Close the lid, set the machine to "Dough" and press Start. Meanwhile, grease a 23cm/9in loose-bottomed springform tin fitted with a tube base, or a ring mould, and set aside.

When the dough is ready, remove it from the machine, knock it back on a lightly floured surface, then divide it into 12 equal portions and roll each piece into a ball.

Combine the melted butter, egg, cheese, garlic, salt and dried herbs in a small bowl, mixing well. Dip the dough balls into the mixture, coating them liberally all over, then arrange them in a single layer in the tin. Drizzle over any remaining butter mixture. Cover and leave to rise in a warm place until doubled in size.

Preheat the oven to 190°C/375°F/gas 5. Bake for 30–40 minutes, or until the bread is risen and golden brown. Turn out and cool on a wire rack. Pull the rolls apart to serve warm or cold.

CHEESE & OLIVE BREAD

PREPARATION TIME 10 minutes

COOKING TIME varies according to bread machine

MAKES 1 loaf (serves 8–10)

300ml/10½ fl oz/1¼ cups water

1 tbsp extra virgin olive oil

450g/1lb/3¼ cups strong white flour

70g/2½oz/½ cup freshly grated Parmesan cheese

2 tsp dried Italian herb seasoning

1½ tsp salt

2 tsp caster/superfine sugar

1 tsp fast-action dried yeast/instant dry yeast

55g/2oz/⅓ cup mixed pitted black and green olives (drained weight), chopped

Pour the water into the bread pan, then add the oil. Sprinkle over the flour, covering the liquid completely. Sprinkle over the Parmesan cheese and dried herb seasoning. Place the salt and sugar in separate corners of the pan. Make a small indent in the centre of the flour and add the yeast.

Close the lid, set the machine to "Basic White"/ "Normal", with "Raisin", if available (or equivalent), then select the loaf size and crust type. Press Start.

Add the mixed olives when the machine makes a sound (beeps) to add extra ingredients during the kneading cycle (or add 5 minutes before the end of the kneading cycle).

After baking, remove the bread pan from the machine and turn the loaf out onto a wire rack to cool. Serve in slices.

GOLDEN CHEESY BREADS

PREPARATION TIME 15 minutes, plus mixing & kneading time in bread machine, plus rising
COOKING TIME 20–25 minutes
MAKES 4 small loaves (each loaf serves 1–2)

300ml/10½ fl oz/1¼ cups milk (at room temperature), plus extra for glazing
450g/1lb/3¼ cups strong white flour
1 tsp mustard powder
200g/7oz/1⅔ cups grated Gouda cheese
1¼ tsp salt
1½ tsp caster/superfine sugar
25g/1oz/2 tbsp butter, diced
1½ tsp fast-action dried yeast/instant dry yeast

Pour the milk into the bread pan. Sprinkle over the flour, covering the milk completely, then sprinkle over the mustard powder and two-thirds of the cheese. Place the salt, sugar and butter in separate corners of the pan. Make a small indent in the centre of the flour and add the yeast. Close the lid, set the machine to "Dough" and press Start.

Meanwhile, grease or flour two baking sheets and set aside. When the dough is ready, remove it from the machine, knock it back on a lightly floured surface, then divide into four equal portions. Shape each portion into a round or oval and place on the baking sheets. Cover and leave to rise in a warm place until doubled in size.

Preheat the oven to 200°C/400°F/gas 6. Lightly brush the tops of the loaves with a little milk, then sprinkle over the remaining cheese.

Bake for 20–25 minutes, or until the bread is risen and golden brown and sounds hollow when tapped underneath. Cover the loaves loosely with foil towards the end of the cooking time if they are browning too much. Transfer to a wire rack to cool. Serve warm or cold.

SESAME RING BREADS

PREPARATION TIME 15 minutes, plus mixing & kneading time in bread machine, plus rising
COOKING TIME 10–15 minutes
MAKES 8 ring breads

250ml/9fl oz/1 cup water
3 tbsp unrefined or cold-pressed sesame oil
1 tbsp clear honey
450g/1lb/3¼ cups strong white flour
1½ tsp salt
2 tsp caster/superfine sugar
1 sachet (7g/¼oz) fast-action dried yeast/
instant dry yeast
beaten egg, for glazing
sesame seeds, for sprinkling

Pour the water into a bowl, add the oil and honey and whisk well. Pour the mixture into the bread pan. Sprinkle over the flour, covering the liquid completely. Place the salt and sugar in separate corners of the pan. Make a small indent in the centre of the flour and add the yeast. Close the lid, set the machine to "Dough" and press Start.

Meanwhile, grease or flour two baking sheets and set aside. When the dough is ready, remove it from the machine, knock it back on a lightly floured surface, then divide the dough into eight equal portions.

Roll each portion into a sausage or rope shape about 30cm/12in long. Form each rope of dough into a ring and press the ends firmly together to seal. Place on the baking sheets, spacing them well apart. Cover and leave to rise in a warm place until doubled in size.

Preheat the oven to 200°C/400°F/gas 6. Lightly brush the dough rings with a little beaten egg and sprinkle with sesame seeds.

Bake for about 10–15 minutes, or until risen and golden brown. Transfer to a wire rack to cool. Serve warm.

HERBY POLENTA BREAD

PREPARATION TIME 10 minutes

COOKING TIME varies according to bread machine

MAKES 1 loaf (serves 10)

300ml/10½ fl oz/1¼ cups water

3 tbsp clear honey

3 tbsp chopped fresh mixed herbs, such as flat-leaf parsley, chives and basil

55g/2oz/⅓ cup polenta/cornmeal

350g/12oz/2⅔ cups strong wholemeal/wholewheat flour

115g/4oz/¾ cup plus 1 tbsp strong white flour

1½ tsp salt

25g/1oz/2 tbsp butter, diced

1½ tsp fast-action dried yeast/instant dry yeast

Pour the water into the bread pan, then add the honey. Sprinkle over the chopped herbs and polenta, then sprinkle over each type of flour in turn, covering the liquid completely.

Place the salt and butter in separate corners of the pan. Make a small indent in the centre of the flour and add the yeast.

Close the lid, set the machine to "Wholewheat" (or equivalent), then select the loaf size and crust type. Press Start.

After baking, remove the bread pan from the machine and turn the loaf out onto a wire rack to cool. Serve in slices.

VARIATION Use maple syrup in place of the honey.

CHEESE & BACON BREAD

PREPARATION TIME 20 minutes

COOKING TIME varies according to bread machine

MAKES 1 loaf (serves 10)

350ml/12fl oz/1½ cups water

500g/1lb 2oz/3½ cups strong brown flour

1½ tbsp skimmed milk powder

1½ tsp salt

1 tbsp granulated sugar

1 tsp fast-action dried yeast/instant dry yeast

85g/3oz/⅓ cup chopped cold cooked lean smoked back bacon

85g/3oz/⅔ cup grated mature/sharp Cheddar cheese

Pour the water into the bread pan. Sprinkle over the flour, covering the water completely. Sprinkle the milk powder over the flour. Place the salt and sugar in separate corners of the pan. Make a small indent in the centre of the flour and add the yeast.

Close the lid, set the machine to "Basic White"/ "Normal", with "Raisin", if available (or equivalent), then select the loaf size and crust type. Press Start.

Combine the bacon and cheese. Add the bacon and cheese mixture when the machine makes a sound (beeps) to add extra ingredients during the kneading cycle (or add 5 minutes before the end of the kneading cycle).

After baking, remove the bread pan from the machine and turn the loaf out onto a wire rack to cool. Serve in slices.

SAUSAGE & SALSA POPOVERS

PREPARATION TIME 20 minutes, plus mixing & kneading time in bread machine, plus rising

COOKING TIME 15–20 minutes

MAKES 10 popovers

325ml/11fl oz/1⅓ cups warm water
(or according to bread mix packet instructions)

500g/1lb 2oz packet white bread mix

55g/2oz/½ cup finely grated mature/sharp
Cheddar cheese

a good pinch of cayenne pepper

10 cold cooked skinless thick sausages of your
choice (pork, beef, herby, spicy, etc.)

20 tsp tomato salsa (2 tsp per popover)

beaten egg, for glazing

Pour the correct amount of water into the bread pan. Sprinkle over the bread mix, covering the water completely, then sprinkle over the cheese and cayenne pepper. Close the lid, set the machine to "Dough" and press Start.

Meanwhile, grease or flour two baking sheets and set aside. When the dough is ready, remove it from the machine and knock it back on a lightly floured surface. Roll out the dough to form a rectangle measuring 50 x 20cm/20 x 8in, then cut into ten 10cm/4in squares.

Place one sausage diagonally across one square of dough, then spread 2 teaspoons of salsa over the sausage. Fold the two uncovered corners of the dough square over the sausage, pinching the edges together and pressing them down gently to seal (you will still be able to see both ends of the sausage).

Repeat with the remaining dough squares, sausages and salsa, to make a total of 10 popovers. Place, seam-side up, on the baking sheets, cover and leave to rise in a warm place for about 30 minutes, or until doubled in size.

Preheat the oven to 200°C/400°F/gas 6. Lightly brush the popovers with a little beaten egg, then bake for 15–20 minutes, or until risen and golden brown. Transfer to a wire rack to cool. Serve warm or cold.

BASIC & EVERYDAY ROLLS

Bread rolls make for a quick and tasty treat any time of day; from warm, crusty rolls for breakfast to a wholesome, filling lunch or an easy teatime snack. In this chapter you will find a selection of delicious rolls, baps, knots and bagels that are ideal for everyday eating.

Try Soft Wholemeal Rolls, Floury White Baps or Malted Country Rolls – perfect for lunchboxes. For breads with added flavours, choose from Rosemary Ciabatta Rolls and Golden Cheddar Twists, or seeded breads such as Sesame Bagels and Poppyseed Knots. And for a European twist, try Petits Pains au Lait, Sun-dried Tomato Rolls or Mediterranean Olive Bread Rolls.

BREAKFAST ROLLS

PREPARATION TIME 15 minutes, plus mixing & kneading time in bread machine, plus rising

COOKING TIME 15–20 minutes

MAKES 10–12 rolls

150ml/5fl oz/⅔ cup milk (at room temperature), plus extra for glazing

150ml/5fl oz/⅔ cup water

450g/1lb/3¼ cups strong white flour, plus extra for dusting

1½ tsp salt

2 tsp caster/superfine sugar

25g/1oz/2 tbsp butter, diced

1½ tsp fast-action dried yeast/instant dry yeast

Pour the milk and water into the bread pan. Sprinkle over the flour, covering the liquid completely. Place the salt, sugar and butter in separate corners of the pan. Make a small indent in the centre of the flour and add the yeast. Close the lid, set the machine to "Dough" and press Start.

Meanwhile, grease or flour two baking sheets and set aside. When the dough is ready, remove it from the machine, knock it back on a lightly floured surface, then divide it into 10 or 12 equal portions.

Shape each portion of the dough into a round or oval and place on the baking sheets, spacing them well apart. Cover and leave to rise in a warm place for about 30 minutes, or until doubled in size.

Preheat the oven to 200°C/400°F/gas 6. Lightly brush the rolls with milk and dust with flour. Bake for 15–20 minutes, or until lightly browned. Transfer to a wire rack to cool. Serve warm or cold.

DINNER ROLLS

PREPARATION TIME 15 minutes, plus mixing & kneading time in bread machine, plus rising

COOKING TIME 15–20 minutes

MAKES 12 rolls

250ml/9fl oz/1 cup milk (at room temperature)

1 egg, beaten

450g/1lb/3¼ cups strong white flour

2 tsp salt

2 tsp caster/superfine sugar

55g/2oz/4 tbsp butter, diced

1 sachet (7g/¼oz) fast-action dried yeast/ instant dry yeast

poppy seeds or sesame seeds, for sprinkling (optional)

Pour the milk into a bowl, add the egg and whisk together. Pour the mixture into the bread pan. Sprinkle over the flour, covering the liquid completely. Add the salt, sugar and butter in separate corners of the pan. Make a small indent in the centre of the flour and add the yeast. Close the lid, set the machine to "Dough" and press Start.

Meanwhile, grease or flour two baking sheets and set aside. When the dough is ready, remove it from the machine, knock it back on a lightly floured surface, then divide it into 12 equal portions.

Form each portion of the dough into a round, oval or baton, or shape into a long roll or rope and tie loosely in a single knot, pulling the ends through.

Place the rolls on the baking sheets, spacing them well apart. Cover and leave to rise in a warm place for about 30 minutes, or until doubled in size.

Preheat the oven to 220°C/425°F/gas 7. Lightly brush the tops of the rolls with a little water and sprinkle with poppy or sesame seeds, if desired. Bake for 15–20 minutes, or until risen and golden brown. Transfer to a wire rack to cool. Serve warm or cold.

SOFT WHOLEMEAL ROLLS

PREPARATION TIME 15 minutes, plus mixing & kneading time in bread machine, plus rising
COOKING TIME 10–15 minutes
MAKES 10–12 rolls

150ml/5fl oz/⅔ cup water

150ml/5fl oz/⅔ cup milk (at room temperature)

350g/12oz/2⅔ cups strong wholemeal/ wholewheat flour, plus extra for dusting

115g/4oz/¾ cup plus 1 tbsp strong white flour

1½ tsp salt

2 tsp caster/superfine sugar

25g/1oz/2 tbsp butter, diced

1½ tsp fast-action dried yeast/instant dry yeast

Pour the water and milk into the bread pan. Sprinkle over each type of flour in turn, covering the liquid completely. Add the salt, sugar and butter in separate corners of the pan. Make a small indent in the centre of the flour and add the yeast. Close the lid, set the machine to "Dough" and press Start.

Meanwhile, grease or flour two baking sheets and set aside. When the dough is ready, remove it from the machine, knock it back on a lightly floured surface, then divide it into 10 or 12 equal portions.

Shape each portion of the dough into a round or oval, then press each one down firmly with the heel of your hand and release. Place the rolls on the baking sheets, spacing them well apart, then cover and leave to rise in a warm place for about 30 minutes, or until doubled in size.

Preheat the oven to 220°C/425°F/gas 7. Lightly dust the tops of the rolls with wholemeal/ wholewheat flour. Bake for 10–15 minutes, or until lightly browned. Transfer to a wire rack to cool. Serve warm or cold.

FLOURY WHITE BAPS

PREPARATION TIME 15 minutes, plus mixing & kneading time in bread machine, plus rising

COOKING TIME 15 minutes

MAKES 10 baps

200ml/7fl oz/scant 1 cup milk (at room temperature), plus extra for glazing

130ml/4fl oz/½ cup water

450g/1lb/3¼ cups strong white flour, plus extra for dusting

1½ tsp salt

2 tsp caster/superfine sugar

1 tsp fast-action dried yeast/instant dry yeast

Pour the milk and water into the bread pan. Sprinkle over the flour, covering the liquid completely. Place the salt and sugar in separate corners of the pan. Make a small indent in the centre of the flour and add the yeast. Close the lid, set the machine to "Dough" and press Start.

Meanwhile, grease or flour two baking sheets and set aside. When the dough is ready, remove it from the machine, knock it back on a lightly floured surface, then divide it into 10 equal portions.

Shape each portion of the dough into a flat round, each about 9cm/3½in in diameter, and place on the baking sheets, spacing them well apart. Cover and leave to rise in a warm place for about 30 minutes, or until doubled in size.

Preheat the oven to 200°C/400°F/gas 6. Gently press the centre of each bap to release any large air bubbles. Lightly brush the baps with milk and dust with flour.

Bake for about 15 minutes, or until lightly browned. Dust with a little more flour, then transfer to a wire rack to cool. Serve warm or cold.

SCOTTISH BAPS

PREPARATION TIME 15 minutes, plus mixing & kneading time in bread machine, plus rising

COOKING TIME 15–20 minutes

MAKES 10 baps

150ml/5fl oz/²⁄₃ cup milk (at room temperature), plus extra for glazing

150ml/5fl oz/²⁄₃ cup water

450g/1lb/3¼ cups strong white flour, plus extra for dusting

1½ tsp salt

2 tsp caster/superfine sugar

1½ tsp fast-action dried yeast/instant dry yeast

Pour the milk and water into the bread pan. Sprinkle over the flour, covering the liquid completely. Place the salt and sugar in separate corners of the pan. Make a small indent in the centre of the flour and add the yeast. Close the lid, set the machine to "Dough" and press Start.

Meanwhile, grease or flour two baking sheets and set aside. When the dough is ready, remove it from the machine, knock it back on a lightly floured surface, then divide it into 10 equal portions.

Roll or pat each portion of the dough into a round or oval about 1cm/½in thick. Place on the baking sheets, spacing them well apart, then cover and leave to rise in a warm place for about 30 minutes, or until doubled in size.

Preheat the oven to 200°C/400°F/gas 6. Gently press the centre of each bap to release any large air bubbles. Lightly brush the baps with milk and dust with flour.

Bake for 15–20 minutes, or until lightly browned. Dust the tops with a little more flour, then transfer to a wire rack to cool. Serve warm.

ROSEMARY CIABATTA ROLLS

PREPARATION TIME 20 minutes, plus mixing & kneading time in bread machine, plus rising

COOKING TIME 20 minutes

MAKES about 10 good-sized rolls

350ml/12fl oz/1½ cups water

2 tbsp olive oil

500g/1lb 2oz/3½ cups strong white flour, plus extra for dusting

1 tsp salt

1 tsp granulated sugar

1 tsp fast-action dried yeast/instant dry yeast

1 tbsp finely chopped fresh rosemary, plus extra sprigs to garnish

milk, for glazing

Pour the water into the bread pan, then add the oil. Sprinkle over the flour, covering the liquid completely. Place the salt and sugar in separate corners of the pan. Make a small indent in the centre of the flour and add the yeast. Close the lid, set the machine to "Dough" and press Start.

Meanwhile, grease or flour two baking sheets and set aside. When the dough is ready, remove it from the machine, knock it back on a lightly floured surface, then knead the chopped rosemary evenly into the dough.

Divide the dough into about 10 equal portions. Roll and shape each portion into a round or oval, then flatten them slightly. Place on the baking sheets, spacing them well apart. Cover and leave to rise in a warm place for about 30 minutes, or until doubled in size.

Preheat the oven to 200°C/400°F/gas 6. Brush the tops of the rolls with milk and dust with flour.

Bake for about 20 minutes, or until the rolls are golden brown and sound hollow when tapped underneath. Transfer to a wire rack to cool. Garnish with sprigs of rosemary and serve warm.

PANINI ROLLS

PREPARATION TIME 15 minutes, plus mixing & kneading time in bread machine, plus rising

COOKING TIME 15 minutes

MAKES 12 rolls

265ml/9½fl oz/1 cup plus 1 tbsp water

4 tbsp extra virgin olive oil, plus extra for glazing

450g/1lb/3¼ cups strong white flour

2 tsp salt

2 tsp caster/superfine sugar

1 sachet (7g/¼oz) fast-action dried yeast/
instant dry yeast

Pour the water into the bread pan, then add the oil. Sprinkle over the flour, covering the liquid completely. Place the salt and sugar in separate corners of the pan. Make a small indent in the centre of the flour and add the yeast. Close the lid, set the machine to "Dough" and press Start.

Meanwhile, grease or flour two baking sheets and set aside. When the dough is ready, remove it from the machine, knock it back on a lightly floured surface, then divide it into 12 equal portions.

Shape each portion of the dough into a ball and place on the baking sheets, spacing them well apart. Brush with olive oil, cover and leave to rise in a warm place for 20–30 minutes, or until doubled in size.

Preheat the oven to 200°C/400°F/gas 6. Using a sharp knife, cut a cross in the top of each roll. Bake for about 15 minutes, or until golden brown. Transfer to a wire rack to cool. Serve warm or cold.

MALTED COUNTRY ROLLS

PREPARATION TIME 15 minutes, plus mixing & kneading time in bread machine, plus rising

COOKING TIME 15–20 minutes

MAKES 10–12 rolls

150ml/5fl oz/⅔ cup milk (at room temperature), plus extra for glazing

125ml/4fl oz/½ cup water

1 tbsp malt extract

450g/1lb/3¼ cups strong malted granary/mixed grain flour

2 tsp salt

2 tsp soft light brown sugar

25g/1oz/2 tbsp butter, diced

1½ tsp fast-action dried yeast/instant dry yeast

kibbled or cracked wheat, for sprinkling

Pour the milk and water into the bread pan, then add the malt extract. Sprinkle over the flour, covering the liquid completely. Place the salt, sugar and butter in separate corners of the pan. Make a small indent in the centre of the flour and add the yeast. Close the lid, set the machine to "Dough" and press Start.

Meanwhile, grease or flour two baking sheets and set aside. When the dough is ready, remove it from the machine, knock it back on a lightly floured surface, then divide it into 10 or 12 equal portions.

Shape each portion of the dough into a round or oval and place on the baking sheets, spacing them well apart. Gently press down on each roll to flatten slightly. Cover and leave to rise in a warm place until doubled in size.

Preheat the oven to 200°C/400°F/gas 6. Lightly brush the rolls with milk and sprinkle with kibbled or cracked wheat. Bake for 15–20 minutes, or until lightly browned. Transfer to a wire rack to cool. Serve warm or cold.

GOLDEN CHEDDAR TWISTS

PREPARATION TIME 20 minutes, plus mixing & kneading time in bread machine, plus rising

COOKING TIME 15–20 minutes

MAKES 10 twists

325ml/11fl oz/1⅓ cups warm water
(or according to bread mix packet instructions)
500g/1lb 2oz packet white bread mix
1 tsp mustard powder
a few turns of freshly ground black pepper
115g/4oz/scant 1 cup finely grated mature/
sharp Cheddar cheese
beaten egg or milk, for glazing

Pour the correct amount of water into the bread pan. Sprinkle over the bread mix, covering the water completely. Sprinkle over the mustard powder and black pepper, then sprinkle over 85g/3oz/¾ cup of the cheese. Close the lid, set the machine to "Dough" and press Start.

Grease or flour two baking sheets and set aside. When the dough is ready, remove it from the machine, knock it back on a lightly floured surface, then divide it into 10 equal portions.

Roll each portion of the dough into a long sausage or rope shape and gently tie each one loosely in a single knot. Place on the baking sheets, spacing them well apart, brush with beaten egg or milk and sprinkle with the remaining cheese. Cover and leave to rise in a warm place until doubled in size.

Preheat the oven to 200°C/400°F/gas 6. Bake the rolls for 15–20 minutes, or until risen and golden brown. Transfer to a wire rack to cool. Serve warm or cold.

SUN-DRIED TOMATO ROLLS

PREPARATION TIME 20 minutes, plus mixing & kneading time in bread machine, plus rising

COOKING TIME 20 minutes

MAKES about 10 good-sized rolls

350ml/12fl oz/1½ cups water

2 tbsp oil from a jar of sun-dried tomatoes

500g/1lb 2oz/3½ cups strong white flour, plus extra for dusting

1 tsp salt

1 tsp granulated sugar

1 tsp fast-action dried yeast/instant dry yeast

115g/4oz/1 cup sun-dried tomatoes in oil (drained weight), patted dry and chopped

milk, for glazing

Pour the water into the bread pan, then add the oil. Sprinkle over the flour, covering the liquid completely. Place the salt and sugar in separate corners of the pan. Make a small indent in the centre of the flour and add the yeast. Close the lid, set the machine to "Dough" and press Start.

Meanwhile, grease or flour two baking sheets and set aside. When the dough is ready, remove it from the machine, knock it back on a lightly floured surface, then knead the chopped tomatoes evenly into the dough.

Divide the dough into about 10 equal portions. Roll and shape each portion into a round or oval, then flatten slightly. Place on the baking sheets, spacing them well apart. Cover and leave to rise in a warm place for about 30 minutes, or until doubled in size.

Preheat the oven to 200°C/400°F/gas 6. Brush the tops of the rolls with milk and dust with flour. Bake for about 20 minutes, or until the rolls are golden brown and sound hollow when tapped underneath. Transfer to a wire rack to cool. Serve warm.

MEDITERRANEAN OLIVE BREAD ROLLS

PREPARATION TIME 20 minutes, plus mixing & kneading time in bread machine, plus rising

COOKING TIME 20 minutes

MAKES about 10 good-sized rolls

350ml/12fl oz/1½ cups water

2 tbsp extra virgin olive oil, plus extra for glazing

500g/1lb 2oz/3½ cups strong white flour

1 tsp salt

1 tsp granulated sugar

1 tsp fast-action dried yeast/instant dry yeast

115g/4oz/¾ cup pitted black olives (drained weight), chopped

Pour the water into the bread pan, then add the oil. Sprinkle over the flour, covering the liquid completely. Place the salt and sugar in separate corners of the pan. Make a small indent in the centre of the flour and add the yeast. Close the lid, set the machine to "Dough" and press Start.

Meanwhile, grease or flour two baking sheets and set aside. When the dough is ready, remove it from the machine, knock it back on a lightly floured surface, then knead the chopped olives evenly into the dough.

Divide the dough into about 10 equal portions. Roll and shape each portion into a round or oval, then flatten slightly. Place on the baking sheets, spacing them well apart. Cover and leave to rise in a warm place for about 30 minutes, or until doubled in size.

Preheat the oven to 200°C/400°F/gas 6. Brush the tops of the rolls with olive oil. Bake for about 20 minutes, or until the rolls are golden brown and sound hollow when tapped underneath. Transfer to a wire rack to cool. Serve warm.

VARIATION Knead 1–2 tablespoons chopped fresh mixed herbs into the dough with the olives, if desired.

SEEDED KNOTS

PREPARATION TIME 20 minutes, plus mixing & kneading time in bread machine, plus rising

COOKING TIME 15–20 minutes

MAKES 12 knots

340ml/11½fl oz/scant 1½ cups milk (at room temperature)

500g/1lb 2oz/3½ cups strong white flour

2 tsp salt

2 tsp caster/superfine sugar

25g/1oz/2 tbsp butter, diced

1 sachet (7g/¼oz) fast-action dried yeast/instant dry yeast

caraway seeds, pumpkin seeds and poppy seeds, for sprinkling

Pour the milk into the bread pan. Sprinkle over the flour, covering the milk completely. Place the salt, sugar and butter in separate corners of the pan. Make a small indent in the centre of the flour and add the yeast. Close the lid, set the machine to "Dough" and press Start.

Meanwhile, grease or flour two baking sheets and set aside. When the dough is ready, remove it from the machine, knock it back on a lightly floured surface, then divide it into 12 equal portions.

Roll each portion of the dough into a long sausage or rope shape and gently tie each one loosely in a single knot. Place on the baking sheets, spacing them well apart, then cover and leave to rise in a warm place for about 30 minutes, or until doubled in size.

Preheat the oven to 220°C/425°F/gas 7. Lightly brush the rolls with a little water and sprinkle four rolls with caraway seeds, four with pumpkin seeds and four with poppy seeds. Bake for 15–20 minutes, or until risen and golden brown. Transfer to a wire rack to cool. Serve warm or cold.

SESAME BAGELS

PREPARATION TIME 10 minutes, plus mixing & kneading time in bread machine,
plus 10 minutes to shape bagels, plus rising

COOKING TIME 30–35 minutes

MAKES 12 bagels

275ml/9½fl oz/1 cup plus 2 tbsp water

2 tbsp sunflower oil

450g/1lb/3¼ cups strong white flour

1½ tsp salt

1 tbsp caster/superfine sugar

1 sachet (7g/¼oz) fast-action dried yeast/
  instant dry yeast

1 tbsp malt extract

milk or water, for glazing

about 2 tbsp sesame seeds, for sprinkling

Pour the water into the bread pan, then add the oil. Sprinkle over the flour, covering the liquid completely. Place the salt and sugar in separate corners of the pan. Make a small indent in the centre of the flour and add the yeast. Close the lid, set the machine to "Dough" and press Start.

Grease two baking sheets. When the dough is ready, knock it back on a lightly floured surface, then divide it into 12 equal portions.

Shape each portion of the dough into a ball, then, using a floured wooden spoon handle, make a hole through the centre of each ball. Enlarge the holes by pulling the dough outwards a little to form rings (bear in mind that the holes will close slightly when the dough is risen and poached). Place on the baking sheets, cover and leave to rise in a warm place until doubled in size.

Preheat the oven to 200°C/400°F/gas 6. Heat a large pan of water to simmering, then stir in the malt extract. Drop each bagel into the water (three or four at a time) and poach for about 3 minutes, turning once. Remove from the water, drain well, then return the bagels to the baking sheets.

Brush each bagel with a little milk or water and sprinkle the tops with sesame seeds. Bake for about 20 minutes, or until cooked and golden brown. Transfer to a wire rack to cool.

PETITS PAINS AU LAIT

PREPARATION TIME 15 minutes, plus mixing & kneading time in bread machine, plus rising

COOKING TIME 15–20 minutes

MAKES 12 rolls

300ml/10½ fl oz/1¼ cups milk (at room temperature), plus extra for glazing

450g/1lb/3¼ cups strong white flour

1½ tsp salt

1 tbsp caster/superfine sugar

55g/2oz/4 tbsp butter, diced

2 tsp fast-action dried yeast/instant dry yeast

Pour the milk into the bread pan. Sprinkle over the flour, covering the milk completely. Place the salt, sugar and butter in separate corners of the pan. Make a small indent in the centre of the flour and add the yeast. Close the lid, set the machine to "Dough" and press Start.

Meanwhile, grease or flour two baking sheets and set aside. When the dough is ready, remove it from the machine, knock it back on a lightly floured surface, then divide it into 12 equal portions. Shape each portion of the dough into a 13cm/5in long roll, tapered at each end, and place on the baking sheets, spacing them well apart. Cover and leave to rise in a warm place for 20–30 minutes, or until doubled in size.

Preheat the oven to 200°C/400°F/gas 6. Using a sharp knife, slash the top of each roll diagonally several times, then brush with milk. Bake for 15–20 minutes, or until golden brown. Transfer to a wire rack to cool. Serve warm or cold.

POPPYSEED KNOTS

PREPARATION TIME 20 minutes, plus mixing & kneading time in bread machine, plus rising

COOKING TIME 15–20 minutes

MAKES 10 knots

325ml/11fl oz/1⅓ cups warm water (or according to bread mix packet instructions)

500g/1lb 2oz packet white bread mix

beaten egg or milk, for glazing

poppy seeds, for sprinkling

Pour the correct amount of water into the bread pan. Sprinkle over the bread mix, covering the water completely. Close the lid, set the machine to "Dough" and press Start.

Meanwhile, grease or flour two baking sheets and set aside. When the dough is ready, remove it from the machine, knock it back on a lightly floured surface, then divide it into 10 equal portions.

Roll each portion of the dough into a long sausage or rope shape and gently tie each one loosely in a single knot. Place on the baking sheets, spacing them well apart, then brush with beaten egg or milk and sprinkle with poppy seeds. Cover and leave to rise in a warm place until doubled in size.

Preheat the oven to 200°C/400°F/gas 6. Bake the rolls for 15–20 minutes, or until risen and golden brown. Transfer to a wire rack to cool. Serve warm or cold.

FLAT BREADS

Flat breads, whether leavened or unleavened, vary in texture, flavour and shape. They may be crisp or chewy, plain or rich, and most of them are quick and easy to prepare and cook.

Many flat breads provide an ideal accompaniment to numerous dishes; some are great for dipping or mopping up sauces, while others are perfect for filling or wrapping to create a quick supper or snack.

We include a whole variety of tempting flat bread recipes from around the world, ranging from flavourful Spiced Naan Breads and North African Flat Breads to Sun-dried Tomato & Olive Focaccia and Pancetta, Pepper & Olive Pizzas.

PITTA BREADS

PREPARATION TIME 15 minutes, plus mixing & kneading time in bread machine, plus rising
COOKING TIME 10 minutes
MAKES 8 pitta breads

225ml/8fl oz/scant 1 cup water
1 tbsp olive oil
350g/12oz/2⅔ cups strong white flour
1½ tsp salt
1 tsp caster/superfine sugar
1 tsp fast-action dried yeast/instant dry yeast

Pour the water into the bread pan, then add the oil. Sprinkle over the flour, covering the liquid completely. Place the salt and sugar in separate corners of the pan. Make a small indent in the centre of the flour and add the yeast. Close the lid, set the machine to "Basic Dough" or "Pizza Dough" and press Start.

When the dough is ready, remove it from the machine, knock it back on a lightly floured surface, then divide it into eight equal portions.

Roll out each portion of the dough to form a flat oval, about 3–5mm/⅛–¼in thick and about 14–15cm/5½–6in long. Lay the dough ovals on a floured tea towel, cover and leave to rise at normal room temperature for about 30 minutes.

Preheat the oven to 230°C/450°F/gas 8. Put three baking sheets in the oven to heat. Place the pitta breads on the hot baking sheets and bake for about 10 minutes, or until puffed up and golden brown.

Serve warm or wrap in a clean tea towel and leave to cool on a wire rack, then heat under a grill when required. To serve, split open and stuff with your chosen filling.

FOCACCIA BREADS

PREPARATION TIME 15 minutes, plus mixing & kneading time in bread machine, plus rising
COOKING TIME 20–25 minutes
MAKES 8 focaccia breads

240ml/8½fl oz/1 cup water
3 tbsp olive oil, plus extra for drizzling
450g/1lb/3¼ cups strong white flour
1 tsp salt
1½ tsp granulated sugar
1½ tsp fast-action dried yeast/instant dry yeast
coarse sea salt, for sprinkling

Pour the water into the bread pan, then add the oil. Sprinkle over the flour, covering the liquid completely. Place the salt and sugar in separate corners of the pan. Make a small indent in the centre of the flour and add the yeast. Close the lid, set the machine to "Basic Dough" or "Pizza Dough" and press Start.

Meanwhile, grease or flour two baking sheets and set aside. When the dough is ready, remove it from the machine, knock it back on a lightly floured surface, then divide it into eight equal portions.

Roll each portion of the dough into a ball, then flatten each ball into a round about 10cm/4in in diameter, making the edges slightly thicker than the centres. Place on the baking sheets, cover and leave to rise in a warm place for about 30–45 minutes, or until slightly risen.

Preheat the oven to 200°C/400°F/gas 6. Drizzle a little olive oil over each focaccia, sprinkle with sea salt and spray with a little water.

Bake for 20–25 minutes, or until risen and golden brown, spraying with a little water again after the first 5 minutes of cooking. Transfer to a wire rack to cool. Serve warm or cold, whole or cut into quarters.

SUN-DRIED TOMATO & OLIVE FOCACCIA

PREPARATION TIME 20 minutes, plus mixing & kneading time in bread machine, plus rising
COOKING TIME 20–25 minutes
MAKES 1 loaf (serves 6–8)

300ml/10½ fl oz/1¼ cups water
3 tbsp olive oil, plus extra for drizzling
500g/1lb 2oz/3½ cups strong white flour
1 tsp salt
1 tsp granulated sugar
1 tsp fast-action dried yeast/instant dry yeast
55g/2oz/½ cup sun-dried tomatoes in oil (drained weight), patted dry and chopped
55g/2oz/⅓ cup pitted black olives (drained weight), chopped
coarse sea salt, for sprinkling

Pour the water into the bread pan, then add the oil. Sprinkle over the flour, covering the liquid completely. Place the salt and sugar in separate corners of the pan. Make a small indent in the centre of the flour and add the yeast. Close the lid, set the machine to "Basic Raisin Dough" (or equivalent), or "Dough", and press Start.

Add the tomatoes and olives when the machine makes a sound (beeps) to add extra ingredients during the kneading cycle (or add 5 minutes before the end of the kneading cycle).

Meanwhile, grease or flour a baking sheet and set aside. When the dough is ready, remove it from the machine, knock it back on a lightly floured surface, then roll out the dough to form a large, flat oval about 2.5cm/1in thick. Place on the baking sheet, cover and leave to rise in a warm place until doubled in size.

Preheat the oven to 200°C/400°F/gas 6. Using your fingertips, make deep dimples all over the surface of the dough. Drizzle with oil and sprinkle with sea salt.

Bake for 20–25 minutes, or until cooked and golden. Transfer to a wire rack to cool. Serve warm or cold in chunks or slices.

NORTH AFRICAN FLAT BREADS

PREPARATION TIME 10 minutes, plus mixing & kneading time in bread machine, plus rising
COOKING TIME 15–20 minutes
MAKES 8 flat breads

225ml/8fl oz/scant 1 cup water
5 tbsp olive oil, plus extra for glazing
500g/1lb 2oz/3½ cups strong white flour, plus extra for dusting
2 tsp salt
1½ tsp caster/superfine sugar
1½ tsp fast-action dried yeast/instant dry yeast

Pour the water into the bread pan, then add the oil. Sprinkle over the flour, covering the liquid completely. Place the salt and sugar in separate corners of the pan. Make a small indent in the centre of the flour and add the yeast. Close the lid, set the machine to "Basic Dough" or "Pizza Dough" and press Start.

Meanwhile, grease or flour two baking sheets and set aside. When the dough is ready, remove it from the machine, knock it back on a lightly floured surface, then divide it into eight equal portions.

Roll out each portion of the dough to make a flat round about 10cm/4in in diameter. Place on the baking sheets, then cover and leave to rise in a warm place for about 1 hour, or until slightly risen.

Preheat the oven to 230°C/450°F/gas 8. Brush a little oil over the top of each flat bread and dust with a little flour. Bake for 15–20 minutes, or until risen and golden brown. Transfer to a wire rack to cool. Serve warm.

MOROCCAN FLAT BREADS

PREPARATION TIME 15 minutes, plus mixing & kneading time in bread machine, plus resting

COOKING TIME 15–20 minutes

MAKES 4 flat breads

175ml/6fl oz/¾ cup milk (at room temperature)
280g/10oz/2 cups strong white flour
1 tsp fennel seeds
1 tsp salt
2 tsp clear honey
1 tsp fast-action dried yeast/instant dry yeast
beaten egg, for glazing

Pour the milk into the bread pan. Sprinkle over the flour, covering the milk completely, then sprinkle over the fennel seeds. Place the salt and honey in separate corners of the pan. Make a small indent in the centre of the flour and add the yeast. Close the lid, set the machine to "Basic Dough" or "Pizza Dough" and press Start.

Grease or flour two baking sheets and set aside. When the dough is ready, remove it from the machine, knock it back on a lightly floured surface, then divide it into four equal portions.

Roll the dough into rounds about 9cm/3½in in diameter, and about 2cm/¾in thick. Place on the baking sheets, then, using a sharp knife or scissors, cut twelve 1cm/½in deep slashes all around the edge of each dough round at regular intervals. Cover and leave in a warm place for 20 minutes.

Preheat the oven to 220°C/425°F/gas 7. Brush the tops of the dough rounds with beaten egg, then bake for 15–20 minutes, or until the breads are risen slightly and golden brown. Transfer to a wire rack to cool. Serve whole or cut into quarters.

PANCETTA, PEPPER & OLIVE PIZZAS

PREPARATION TIME 30 minutes, plus mixing & kneading time in bread machine

COOKING TIME 20–25 minutes

MAKES 2 pizzas (each pizza serves 4–6)

FOR THE PIZZA DOUGH

280ml/9½fl oz/1 cup plus 2 tbsp water

2 tbsp olive oil

450g/1lb/3¼ cups strong white flour

1 tsp salt

2 tsp caster/superfine sugar

1½ tsp fast-action dried yeast/instant dry yeast

FOR THE TOPPING

2 tbsp olive oil

2 garlic cloves, crushed

225g/8oz/1 cup diced smoked pancetta

2 large red peppers, halved lengthways, deseeded and sliced

400g/14oz can chopped tomatoes with herbs, drained

2 tbsp tomato purée/paste

115–175g/4–6oz/¾–1 heaped cup pitted black olives, drained weight

115g/4oz/¾ cup freshly grated Parmesan cheese

sea salt and freshly ground black pepper

basil leaves, to garnish (optional)

Make the dough. Pour the water into the bread pan, then add the oil. Sprinkle over the flour, covering the liquid completely. Place the salt and sugar in separate corners of the pan. Make a small indent in the centre of the flour and add the yeast. Close the lid, set the machine to "Basic Dough" or "Pizza Dough" and press Start.

Meanwhile, grease or flour two baking sheets and set aside.

Prepare the topping. Heat the oil in a frying pan, add the garlic and sauté for 30 seconds. Add the pancetta and stir-fry over a high heat until it releases its fat and browns lightly. Remove from the pan and set aside. Add the peppers to the pan and sauté until just softened. Remove the pan from the heat and add the pancetta to the peppers.

When the dough is ready, remove it from the machine, knock it back on a lightly floured surface, then divide it in half. Roll out each piece of dough thinly to form a 30cm (12in) round. Transfer each round to a baking sheet.

Preheat the oven to 220°C/425°F/gas 7. Mix together the tomatoes, tomato purée/paste and salt and pepper. Spread this mixture evenly over the pizza bases to within 1cm (½in) of the edge. Spoon the pepper and pancetta mixture evenly over the tomatoes, then scatter the olives over the top. Sprinkle with the Parmesan cheese.

Bake for 20–25 minutes, or until the bases are crisp and the topping is golden. Serve warm, sprinkled with basil leaves, if using.

NAAN BREADS

PREPARATION TIME 10 minutes, plus mixing & kneading time in bread machine, plus resting
COOKING TIME 10–12 minutes
MAKES 4 good-sized naan breads

120ml/4fl oz/½ cup milk (at room temperature)
4 tbsp natural yogurt (at room temperature)
1 tbsp sunflower oil
300g/10½oz/2 cups plus 2 tbsp strong white flour
1 tsp salt
1½ tsp caster/superfine sugar
1 tsp fast-action dried yeast/instant dry yeast
about 3 tbsp melted ghee or butter, for brushing

Pour the milk into a bowl, add the yogurt and oil and whisk well. Pour the mixture into the bread pan. Sprinkle over the flour, covering the liquid completely. Place the salt and sugar in separate corners of the pan. Make a small indent in the centre of the flour and add the yeast. Close the lid, set the machine to "Basic Dough" or "Pizza Dough" and press Start.

When the dough is ready, remove it from the machine, knock it back on a lightly floured surface, then divide it into four equal portions.

Roll out each portion of the dough to form a flat oval or teardrop shape, about 5mm/¼in thick and 23cm/9in long. Cover and leave for 15 minutes.

Preheat the oven to 230°C/450°F/gas 8. Put two baking sheets in the oven to heat. Place the naan breads on the hot baking sheets and brush with melted ghee or butter. Bake for 10–12 minutes, or until puffed up. Wrap loosely in a clean dish towel and serve warm.

SPICED NAAN BREADS

PREPARATION TIME 10 minutes, plus mixing & kneading time in bread machine, plus resting
COOKING TIME 10–12 minutes
MAKES 4 good-sized naan breads

120ml/4fl oz/½ cup milk (at room temperature)

4 tbsp natural yogurt (at room temperature)

1 tbsp sunflower oil

300g/10½oz/2 cups plus 2 tbsp strong white flour

1½ tsp ground coriander

1 tsp ground cumin

1 tsp hot chilli powder

1 tsp salt

1½ tsp caster/superfine sugar

1 tsp fast-action dried yeast/instant dry yeast

about 3 tbsp melted ghee or butter, for brushing

Pour the milk into a bowl, add the yogurt and oil and whisk well. Pour the mixture into the bread pan. Sprinkle over the flour, covering the liquid completely. Mix the ground spices together, then sprinkle them over the flour. Place the salt and sugar in separate corners of the pan. Make a small indent in the centre of the flour and add the yeast. Close the lid, set the machine to "Basic Dough" or "Pizza Dough" and press Start.

When the dough is ready, remove it from the machine, knock it back on a lightly floured surface, then divide it into four equal portions.

Roll out each portion of the dough to form a flat oval or teardrop shape, about 5mm/¼in thick and 23cm/9in long. Cover and leave for 15 minutes.

Preheat the oven to 230°C/450°F/gas 8. Put two baking sheets in the oven to heat. Place the naan breads on the hot baking sheets and brush with melted ghee or butter. Bake for 10–12 minutes, or until puffed up. Wrap loosely in a clean dish towel and serve warm.

GARLIC & CORIANDER NAAN BREADS

PREPARATION TIME 10 minutes, plus mixing & kneading time in bread machine, plus resting

COOKING TIME 10–12 minutes

MAKES 4 good-sized naan breads

120ml/4fl oz/½ cup milk (at room temperature)

4 tbsp natural yogurt (at room temperature)

1 tbsp sunflower oil

300g/10½oz/2 cups plus 2 tbsp strong white flour

1½ tsp ground coriander

1 large garlic clove, crushed

1 tsp salt

1½ tsp caster/superfine sugar

1 tsp fast-action dried yeast/instant dry yeast

about 3 tbsp melted ghee or butter, for brushing

1–2 tsp black onion seeds

1–2 tbsp chopped fresh coriander/cilantro

Pour the milk into a bowl, add the yogurt and oil and whisk well. Pour the mixture into the bread pan. Sprinkle over the flour, covering the liquid completely. Sprinkle the ground coriander and garlic over the flour. Place the salt and sugar in separate corners of the pan. Make a small indent in the centre of the flour and add the yeast. Close the lid, set the machine to "Basic Dough" or "Pizza Dough" and press Start.

When the dough is ready, remove it from the machine, knock it back on a lightly floured surface, then divide it into four equal portions.

Roll out each portion of the dough to form a flat oval or teardrop shape, about 5mm/¼in thick and 23cm/9in long. Cover and leave for 15 minutes.

Preheat the oven to 230°C/450°F/gas 8. Put two baking sheets in the oven to heat. Place the naan breads on the hot baking sheets, brush with melted ghee or butter, then sprinkle with the onion seeds and fresh coriander/cilantro. Bake for 10–12 minutes, or until puffed up. Wrap loosely in a clean dish towel and serve warm.

QUICK BREADS

Quick breads are quick and easy to make compared to many other types of bread: ingredients are simply mixed together and baked, without the need for prolonged kneading or rising periods, creating a range of delicious sweet and savoury breads.

Some quick breads, such as those that have been enriched with butter, eggs or dried fruit, should keep well for several days if wrapped in foil or stored in an airtight container. Others are best served freshly baked and warm from the oven.

We include a wide range of versatile and tasty quick breads to tempt you. Choose from traditional favourites such Golden Gingerbread and Malted Fruit Loaf, or experiment with different flavour combinations such as Cheese & Date Bread or Celery & Walnut Loaf.

GOLDEN GINGERBREAD

PREPARATION TIME 20 minutes, plus cooling

COOKING TIME 1 hour–1 hour 10 minutes

MAKES 1 loaf (serves 8–10)

115g/4oz/½ cup packed soft light brown sugar

85g/3oz/6 tbsp butter

175g/6oz/½ cup golden/light corn syrup

225g/8oz/1⅔ cups plain/all-purpose white flour

a pinch of salt

1 tsp baking powder

2 tsp ground ginger

1 egg, beaten

150ml/5fl oz/⅔ cup milk

Remove the kneading blade from the bread pan. Remove the bread pan from the machine, grease and line the base and sides of the pan and set aside.

Place the sugar, butter and syrup in a small saucepan and heat gently, stirring, until melted and blended. Remove from the heat and cool slightly. Sift the flour, salt, baking powder and ginger into a bowl and make a well in the centre. Mix together the egg and milk and pour into the well along with the melted mixture. Beat together using a wooden spoon until smooth and thoroughly mixed. Pour the mixture into the bread pan.

Place the bread pan in position in the machine and close the lid. Set the machine to "Bake Only" for 60 minutes. Press Start.

After baking, a fine skewer inserted in the centre of the gingerbread should come out clean. If the gingerbread requires further baking, bake on the same setting for a further 5–10 minutes, or until cooked.

Remove the bread pan from the machine using oven gloves, then leave to stand for 5 minutes, before turning the gingerbread out onto a wire rack to cool. Serve warm or cold in slices.

DATE & WALNUT LOAF

PREPARATION TIME 20 minutes, plus 15 minutes standing

COOKING TIME 45–55 minutes

MAKES 1 loaf (serves 10–12)

225g/8oz/1¼ cups pitted dried dates, chopped

150ml/5fl oz/⅔ cup boiling water

85g/3oz/6 tbsp butter, softened

85g/3oz/⅓ cup packed soft light brown sugar

1 egg, beaten

225g/8oz/1⅔ cups self-raising/self-rising white flour

1 tsp baking powder

85g/3oz/⅔ cup walnuts, chopped

Remove the kneading blade from the bread pan. Remove the bread pan from the machine, grease and line the base and sides of the pan and set aside.

Place the dates in a bowl and pour over the boiling water. Stir to mix, then set aside for 15 minutes. Cream the butter and sugar together in a separate bowl until pale and fluffy, then gradually beat in the egg. Fold in the flour, baking powder, walnuts and date mixture, stirring until well mixed. Spoon the mixture into the bread pan and level the surface.

Place the bread pan in position in the machine and close the lid. Set the machine to "Bake Only" for 45 minutes. Press Start.

After baking, a fine skewer inserted in the centre of the loaf should come out clean. If the loaf requires further baking, bake on the same setting for a further 5–10 minutes, or until cooked.

Remove the bread pan from the machine using oven gloves, then leave to stand for 5 minutes, before turning the loaf out onto a wire rack to cool. Serve warm or cold in slices.

CHEESE & DATE BREAD

PREPARATION TIME 20 minutes

COOKING TIME 45–55 minutes

MAKES 1 loaf (serves 8–10)

225g/8oz/1⅔ cups self-raising/
self-rising white flour

a pinch of salt

55g/2oz/4 tbsp butter, diced

85g/3oz/⅔ cup finely grated mature/sharp
Cheddar cheese

115g/4oz/⅔ cup pitted dried dates,
finely chopped

2 eggs

150ml/5fl oz/⅔ cup milk

Remove the kneading blade from the bread pan. Remove the bread pan from the machine, grease and line the base and sides of the pan and set aside.

Sift the flour and salt into a bowl, then lightly rub in the butter until the mixture resembles breadcrumbs. Stir in 70g/2½oz/scant ⅔ cup of the cheese and the dates. Beat the eggs and milk together in a separate bowl, then add to the date mixture and mix well to combine. Spoon the mixture into the bread pan and level the surface. Sprinkle with the remaining cheese.

Place the bread pan in position in the machine and close the lid. Set the machine to "Bake Only" for 45 minutes. Press Start.

After baking, a fine skewer inserted in the centre of the loaf should come out clean. If the loaf requires further baking, bake on the same setting for a further 5–10 minutes, or until cooked.

Remove the bread pan from the machine using oven gloves, then leave to stand for 5 minutes, before turning the loaf out onto a wire rack to cool. Serve warm or cold in slices.

FRUITY HAZELNUT LOAF

PREPARATION TIME 20 minutes, plus 30 minutes soaking

COOKING TIME 1 hour–1 hour 10 minutes

MAKES 1 loaf (serves 10–12)

85g/3oz/½ cup sultanas/golden raisins

85g/3oz/½ cup ready-to-eat dried apricots, roughly chopped

85g/3oz/1⅓ cups bran

300ml/10½fl oz/1¼ cups milk

115g/4oz/¾ cup plus 1 tbsp self-raising / self-rising white flour

a pinch of salt

115g/4oz/¾ cup plus 1 tbsp self-raising/ self-rising wholemeal/wholewheat flour

55g/2oz/4 tbsp butter, diced

115g/4oz/scant 1 cup hazelnuts, chopped

115g/4oz/¾ cup demerara/turbinado sugar

1 tsp ground mixed spice/apple pie spice

2 eggs, beaten

Place the sultanas/golden raisins, apricots and bran in a bowl, add the milk and mix well. Cover and leave to soak for 30 minutes. Remove the kneading blade from the bread pan, remove the bread pan from the machine, grease and line the base and sides of the pan and set aside.

Sift the white flour and salt into a bowl, stir in the wholemeal/wholewheat flour, then lightly rub in the butter until the mixture resembles breadcrumbs. Add the bran mixture, hazelnuts, sugar, spice and eggs and mix thoroughly. Spoon the mixture into the bread pan and level the surface.

Place the bread pan in position in the machine and close the lid. Set the machine to "Bake Only" for 60 minutes. Press Start.

After baking, a fine skewer inserted in the centre of the loaf should come out clean. If the loaf requires further baking, bake on the same setting for a further 5–10 minutes, or until cooked.

Remove the bread pan from the machine using oven gloves, then leave to stand for 5 minutes, before turning the loaf out onto a wire rack to cool. Serve warm or cold in slices.

BANANA & HONEY LOAF

PREPARATION TIME 20 minutes

COOKING TIME 1 hour–1 hour 10 minutes

MAKES 1 loaf (serves 8–10)

115g/4oz/½ cup butter, softened

115g/4oz/½ cup packed soft light brown sugar

115g/4oz/⅓ cup thick (set) honey

2 eggs, beaten

225g/8oz/1⅔ cups self-raising/self-rising white or wholemeal/wholewheat flour

½ tsp ground nutmeg or cinnamon

2 large bananas

a squeeze of lemon juice

Remove the kneading blade from the bread pan. Remove the bread pan from the machine, grease and line the base and sides of the pan and set aside.

Place the butter, sugar and honey in a bowl and beat together until light and fluffy. Gradually beat in the eggs, then fold in the flour and nutmeg or cinnamon. Peel the bananas and mash the flesh with a little lemon juice. Fold the mashed bananas into the loaf mixture until well mixed, then spoon the mixture into the bread pan and level the surface.

Place the bread pan in position in the machine and close the lid. Set the machine to "Bake Only" for 60 minutes. Press Start.

After baking, a fine skewer inserted in the centre of the loaf should come out clean. If the loaf requires further baking, bake on the same setting for a further 5–10 minutes, or until cooked.

Remove the bread pan from the machine using oven gloves, then leave to stand for 5 minutes, before turning the loaf out onto a wire rack to cool. Serve warm or cold in slices.

MALTED FRUIT LOAF

PREPARATION TIME 20 minutes

COOKING TIME 40–50 minutes

MAKES 1 loaf (serves 10–12)

225g/8oz/1⅔ cups self-raising/
self-rising white flour

1 tsp bicarbonate of soda/baking soda

1 tsp ground mixed spice/apple pie spice

3 tbsp malt extract

2 tbsp golden/light corn syrup

125ml/4fl oz/½ cup milk

1 egg, beaten

140g/5oz/¾ cup sultanas/golden raisins

2 tbsp clear honey, for glazing

Remove the kneading blade from the bread pan. Remove the bread pan from the machine, grease and line the base and sides of the pan and set aside.

Sift the flour, bicarbonate of soda/baking soda and spice into a bowl and set aside. Place the malt extract, syrup and milk in a saucepan and heat gently until melted and blended, stirring occasionally. Remove from the heat and cool slightly, then mix in the egg.

Make a well in the centre of the dry ingredients, then add the melted mixture, mixing well with a wooden spoon. Fold in the sultanas/golden raisins. Spoon the mixture into the bread pan and level the surface.

Place the bread pan in position in the machine and close the lid. Set the machine to "Bake Only" for 40 minutes. Press Start.

After baking, a fine skewer inserted in the centre of the loaf should come out clean. If the loaf requires further baking, bake on the same setting for a further 5–10 minutes, or until cooked.

Remove the bread pan from the machine using oven gloves, then leave to stand for 5 minutes, before turning the loaf out onto a wire rack to cool. While the loaf is still warm, brush it twice with honey to glaze. Serve warm or cold in slices.

CELERY & WALNUT LOAF

PREPARATION TIME 25 minutes

COOKING TIME 45–55 minutes

MAKES 1 loaf (serves 8–10)

225g/8oz/1⅔ cups self-raising/
self-rising white flour

1 tsp baking powder

55g/2oz/4 tbsp butter, diced

2 celery stalks, finely chopped

55g/2oz/½ cup walnuts, finely chopped

85g/3oz/⅔ cup finely grated mature/sharp
Cheddar cheese

1 egg, beaten

about 4 tbsp milk

sea salt and freshly ground black pepper

Remove the kneading blade from the bread pan. Remove the bread pan from the machine, grease and line the base and sides of the pan and set aside.

Sift the flour and baking powder into a bowl, then lightly rub in the butter until the mixture resembles breadcrumbs. Stir in the celery, walnuts, cheese and salt and pepper, and mix well. Mix in the egg and enough milk to form a soft, but not sticky, dough. Turn the dough onto a lightly floured surface and knead gently until smooth. Shape the dough to fit the bread pan and place it in the pan.

Place the bread pan in position in the machine and close the lid. Set the machine to "Bake Only" for 45 minutes. Press Start.

After baking, a fine skewer inserted in the centre of the loaf should come out clean. If the loaf requires further baking, bake on the same setting for a further 5–10 minutes, or until cooked.

Remove the bread pan from the machine using oven gloves, then leave to stand for 5 minutes, before turning the loaf out onto a wire rack to cool. Serve warm or cold in slices, spread with butter.

FRUIT & SPICE BREAD

PREPARATION TIME 20 minutes

COOKING TIME 1 hour–1 hour 10 minutes

MAKES 1 loaf (serves 10–12)

225g/8oz/1²⁄₃ cups self-raising/
self-rising white flour

½ tsp bicarbonate of soda/baking soda

1 tbsp ground mixed spice/apple pie spice

115g/4oz/½ cup packed soft light brown sugar

115g/4oz/²⁄₃ cup sultanas/golden raisins

115g/4oz/²⁄₃ cup raisins

115g/4oz/²⁄₃ cup currants

115g/4oz/²⁄₃ cup ready-to-eat dried apricots,
finely chopped

2 eggs

150ml/5fl oz/²⁄₃ cup milk

Remove the kneading blade from the bread pan. Remove the bread pan from the machine, grease and line the base and sides of the pan and set aside.

Sift the flour, bicarbonate of soda/baking soda and spice into a bowl. Add the sugar and dried fruit and mix well. Beat the eggs and milk together and add to the fruit mixture. Beat until thoroughly mixed. Spoon the mixture into the pan and level the surface.

Place the bread pan in position in the machine and close the lid. Set the machine to "Bake Only" for 60 minutes. Press Start.

After baking, a fine skewer inserted in the centre of the loaf should come out clean. If the loaf requires further baking, bake on the same setting for a further 5–10 minutes, or until cooked.

Remove the bread pan from the machine using oven gloves, then leave to stand for 5 minutes, before turning the loaf out onto a wire rack to cool. Serve warm or cold in slices.

SPECIALITY & FESTIVE BREADS

Speciality breads are made from yeasted doughs that are enriched with a combination of other ingredients, such as eggs, sugar, butter, dried fruit or chocolate. Enriched breads, both sweet and savoury, vary in texture from soft and airy loaves with a rich and buttery flavour, to deliciously light and flaky, melt-in-the-mouth yeasted pastries, all of which are hard to resist.

Some speciality breads, such as Challah, Stollen and Panettone, are traditionally baked to celebrate a particular festival or celebration.

We include a delicious selection of enriched, speciality breads from all over the world, among them Orange & Cinnamon Brioche and Pains au Chocolat, as well as tempting delights such as Croissants, Doughnuts and Coconut Bread. We also include some simpler enriched dough recipes such as Devonshire Splits, Bath Buns and Chelsea Buns.

PARADISE PLAIT

PREPARATION TIME 20 minutes, plus mixing & kneading time in bread machine, plus rising
COOKING TIME 45–50 minutes
MAKES 1 loaf (serves 10)

165ml/5½fl oz/⅔ cup milk (at room
  temperature)

2 large eggs, lightly beaten

450g/1lb/3¼ cups strong white flour

½ tsp salt

55g/2oz/¼ cup caster/superfine sugar

55g/2oz/4 tbsp butter, diced, plus 25g/1oz/
  2 tbsp butter, melted

1 sachet (7g/¼oz) fast-action dried yeast/
  instant dry yeast

55g/2oz/⅓ cup dried pineapple, chopped

115g/4oz/⅔ cup ready-to-eat dried pears,
  chopped

55g/2oz/⅓ cup blanched almonds, chopped

sifted icing/confectioners' sugar, for dusting

Whisk the milk and eggs together in a bowl and pour into the bread pan. Sprinkle over the flour, covering the liquid completely. Place the salt, caster/superfine sugar and diced butter in separate corners of the pan. Make a small indent in the centre of the flour and add the yeast. Close the lid, set the machine to "Basic Raisin Dough" (or equivalent), or "Dough", and press Start.

Add the pineapple, pears and almonds when the machine makes a sound (beeps) to add extra ingredients during the kneading cycle (or add 5 minutes before the end of the kneading cycle). Meanwhile, grease a baking sheet and set aside.

When the dough is ready, remove it from the machine, knock it back on a lightly floured surface, then divide the dough into three equal pieces. Roll each piece of dough into a long sausage or rope shape, about 30cm/12in long. Plait the dough ropes together, pressing them together at both ends to seal. Place on the baking sheet. Cover and leave to rise in a warm place until almost doubled in size.

Preheat the oven to 190°C/375°F/gas 5. Bake the plait for about 45–50 minutes, or until risen and golden brown, covering it loosely with foil towards the end of the cooking time if the top is browning too quickly. Transfer to a wire rack to cool slightly, then brush with the melted butter and dust with icing/confectioners' sugar. Serve warm or cold in slices.

DEVONSHIRE SPLITS

PREPARATION TIME 15 minutes, plus mixing & kneading time in bread machine, plus rising

COOKING TIME 15 minutes

MAKES 10 Devonshire splits

210ml/7½fl oz/¾ cup plus 2 tbsp milk (at room temperature)

350g/12oz/2⅔ cups strong white flour

½ tsp salt

40g/1½oz/3½ tbsp caster/superfine sugar

40g/1½oz/3 tbsp butter, diced

1½ tsp fast-action dried yeast/instant dry yeast

strawberry or raspberry jam and clotted cream, to serve

sifted icing/confectioners' sugar, for dusting

Pour the milk into the bread pan. Sprinkle over the flour, covering the milk completely. Place the salt, caster/superfine sugar and butter in separate corners of the pan. Make a small indent in the centre of the flour and add the yeast. Close the lid, set the machine to "Dough" and press Start.

Meanwhile, grease two baking sheets and set aside. When the dough is ready, remove it from the machine, knock it back on a lightly floured surface, then divide the dough into 10 equal portions and roll each portion into a ball. Place the dough balls on the baking sheets and flatten them slightly. Cover and leave to rise in a warm place until doubled in size.

Preheat the oven to 220°C/425°F/gas 7. Bake the buns for about 15 minutes, or until they feel soft and sound hollow when tapped underneath. Transfer to a wire rack to cool.

Split each bun at an angle and fill with jam and cream. Dust with icing/confectioners' sugar just before serving.

PESTO PARMESAN PULL-APART

PREPARATION TIME 20 minutes, plus mixing & kneading time in bread machine, plus rising

COOKING TIME 30–35 minutes

MAKES 1 loaf (serves 16)

315ml/10½ fl oz/1¼ cups water

450g/1lb/3¼ cups strong white flour

1¼ tsp salt

1½ tsp caster/superfine sugar

1½ tsp fast-action dried yeast/instant dry yeast

3 tbsp ready-made green pesto sauce

40g/1½oz/¼ cup freshly grated Parmesan cheese

beaten egg, for glazing

Pour the water into the bread pan. Sprinkle over the flour, covering the water completely. Place the salt and sugar in separate corners of the pan. Make a small indent in the centre of the flour and add the yeast. Close the lid, set the machine to "Dough" and press Start.

Meanwhile, grease a deep 23cm/9in round cake tin and set aside. When the dough is ready, remove it from the machine, knock it back on a lightly floured surface, then roll out the dough to form a 40 x 28cm/16 x 11in rectangle.

Spread the pesto sauce evenly over the dough, then sprinkle with the Parmesan cheese. Starting from a long side, roll up the dough fairly tightly like a Swiss roll. Cut into 16 even slices, then place the rolls, cut-side up, in a decreasing circular pattern in the cake tin. Cover and leave to rise in a warm place until doubled in size.

Preheat the oven to 200°C/400°F/gas 6. Brush the spirals with beaten egg, then bake for 30–35 minutes, or until deep golden brown. Cool slightly in the tin, then turn out onto a wire rack to cool. Pull the rolls apart to serve and serve warm or cold.

CHEESE & HERB TEAR 'N' SHARE

PREPARATION TIME 15 minutes, plus mixing & kneading time in bread machine, plus rising
COOKING TIME 40 minutes
MAKES 1 loaf (serves 12)

325ml/11fl oz/1⅓ cups warm water
(or according to bread mix packet instructions)
500g/1lb 2oz packet white bread mix
100g/3½ oz/7 tbsp butter, melted
1 large egg, lightly beaten
25g/1oz/2 tbsp freshly grated Parmesan cheese
2 garlic cloves, crushed
½ tsp salt
¼ tsp freshly ground black pepper
2 tsp dried herbes de Provence

Pour the correct amount of water into the bread pan. Sprinkle over the bread mix, covering the water completely. Close the lid, set the machine to "Dough" and press Start.

Meanwhile, grease a deep 20cm/8in round cake tin and set aside. When the dough is ready, remove it from the machine, knock it back on a lightly floured surface, then divide the dough into 12 equal portions and roll each portion into a ball.

Combine the melted butter, egg, Parmesan cheese, garlic, salt, black pepper and dried herbs in a small bowl. Dip the dough balls into the butter mixture, coating them liberally all over, then arrange them in a single layer in the cake tin. Drizzle over any remaining butter mixture. Cover and leave to rise in a warm place for about 45 minutes, or until doubled in size.

Preheat the oven to 190°C/375°F/gas 5. Bake the loaf for about 40 minutes, or until golden brown. Turn out and cool on a wire rack. Pull the rolls apart to serve and serve warm or cold.

MONKEY BREAD

PREPARATION TIME 25 minutes, plus overnight soaking, plus mixing & kneading time
in bread machine, plus rising

COOKING TIME 40 minutes

MAKES 1 loaf (serves 16)

115g/4oz/⅔ cup sultanas/golden raisins

4 tbsp brandy

175ml/6fl oz/¾ cup milk (at room temperature)

1 large egg, lightly beaten

450g/1lb/3¼ cups strong white flour

½ tsp salt

2 tsp caster/superfine sugar

1 sachet (7g/¼ oz) fast-action dried yeast/
    instant dry yeast

115g/4oz/scant 1 cup walnuts, finely chopped

1½ tsp ground mixed spice/apple pie spice

115g/4oz/½ cup packed soft light
    brown sugar

85g/3oz/6 tbsp butter, melted

Place the sultanas/golden raisins in a bowl, add the brandy and stir. Leave to soak overnight.

Pour the milk and 3½ tablespoons water into a bowl, add the egg and whisk well. Pour the mixture into the bread pan. Sprinkle over the flour, covering the liquid completely. Place the salt and caster/superfine sugar in separate corners of the pan. Make a small indent in the centre of the flour and add the yeast. Close the lid, set the machine to "Dough" and press Start.

Meanwhile, grease a 23cm/9in loose-bottomed springform tin fitted with a tube base, or a ring mould, and set aside. Mix the walnuts, spice and brown sugar in a bowl and set aside. Put the melted butter into a separate small bowl and set aside.

When the dough is ready, remove it from the machine, knock it back on a lightly floured surface, then divide the dough into 32 pieces and roll each piece into a ball.

Dip each ball of dough into the melted butter, then roll in the walnut mixture, coating it completely. Place half the coated balls in the tin, spacing them slightly apart. Spoon over the soaked sultanas/golden raisins and any remaining walnut mixture. Top with the rest of the coated dough balls and drizzle over any remaining butter. Cover and leave to rise in a warm place for about 45 minutes, or until doubled in size.

Preheat the oven to 190°C/375°F/gas 5. Bake the loaf for about 40 minutes, or until risen and golden brown. Cool in the tin for 10 minutes, then invert onto a serving plate. Pull the rolls apart to serve and serve warm or cold.

COCONUT BREAD

330ml/11fl oz/1⅓ cups milk (at room temperature)

1 tsp vanilla extract

450g/1lb/3¼ cups strong white flour

55g/2oz/½ cup desiccated/dried shredded coconut

1½ tsp salt

1 tbsp caster/superfine sugar

15g/½oz/1 tbsp butter, diced

1½ tsp fast-action dried yeast/instant dry yeast

Pour the milk into the bread pan and add the vanilla extract. Sprinkle over the flour, covering the milk completely, then sprinkle over the coconut. Place the salt, sugar and butter in separate corners of the pan. Make a small indent in the centre of the flour and add the yeast.

Close the lid, set the machine to "Sweet" or "Basic White"/"Normal" (or equivalent), then select the loaf size and crust type. Press Start.

After baking, remove the bread pan from the machine and turn the loaf out onto a wire rack to cool. Serve in slices.

CHALLAH

PREPARATION TIME 20 minutes, plus mixing & kneading time in bread machine, plus rising
COOKING TIME 35–40 minutes
MAKES 1 loaf (serves 10)

155ml/5fl oz/⅔ cup water

5 tbsp olive oil

2 eggs, lightly beaten

500g/1lb 2oz/3½ cups strong white flour

1½ tsp salt

1 tbsp caster/superfine sugar

1 sachet (7g/¼oz) fast-action dried yeast/
   instant dry yeast

beaten egg, for glazing

sesame or poppy seeds, for sprinkling

Pour the water into a bowl, add the oil and eggs and whisk well. Pour the mixture into the bread pan. Sprinkle over the flour, covering the liquid completely. Place the salt and sugar in separate corners of the pan. Make a small indent in the centre of the flour and add the yeast. Close the lid, set the machine to "Dough" and press Start.

Meanwhile, grease a large baking sheet and set aside. When the dough is ready, remove it from the machine, knock it back on a lightly floured surface, then divide the dough into four equal portions.

Roll each portion of the dough into a rope about 40cm/16in long. Place the ropes of dough side by side and pinch them together at one end.

Starting from the right, make a plait, lifting the first rope over the second and the third rope over the fourth, then placing the fourth rope between the first and second ropes. Repeat and continue, to form a plait, pinching the ends together when you have finished. Tuck the ends under at each end of the plait and place on the baking sheet. Cover and leave to rise in a warm place until doubled in size.

Preheat the oven to 220°C/425°F/gas 7. Brush the dough with beaten egg and sprinkle with sesame or poppy seeds. Bake for 15 minutes, then reduce the oven temperature to 190°C/375°F/gas 5 and bake for a further 20–25 minutes, or until risen and golden brown. Transfer to a wire rack to cool. Serve in slices or wedges.

ORANGE & CINNAMON BRIOCHE

PREPARATION TIME 25 minutes, plus mixing & kneading time in bread machine, plus rising

COOKING TIME 30 minutes

MAKES 1 loaf (serves 12–14)

150g/5½oz/⅔ cup butter

3 large eggs, lightly beaten

2 tbsp milk

1 tbsp finely grated orange zest

450g/1lb/3¼ cups strong white flour

1 tsp ground cinnamon

1 tsp salt

55g/2oz/¼ cup caster/superfine sugar

1 sachet (7g/¼oz) fast-action dried yeast/
    instant dry yeast

beaten egg yolk, for glazing

Melt 75g/2¾oz/5 tablespoons of the butter. Dice the rest. Whisk the melted butter, eggs, milk and orange zest together in a bowl, then pour into the bread pan. Sprinkle over the flour, covering the liquid completely, then sprinkle over the cinnamon. Place the salt, sugar and remaining diced butter in separate corners of the pan. Make a small indent in the centre of the flour and add the yeast. Close the lid, set the machine to "Dough" and press Start.

Grease a 1.7 litre/3 pint brioche tin and set aside. When the dough is ready, remove it from the machine, knock it back on a lightly floured surface, then cut a quarter from the dough and set aside. Knead the remaining larger piece of dough, shape it into a large ball and place it in the tin.

Shape the reserved smaller piece of dough into a pear shape. Make a hollow in the centre of the large round of dough and place the thinner end of the pear-shaped piece of dough into the hollow. Cover and leave to rise in a warm place until the dough nearly reaches the top of the tin.

Preheat the oven to 200°C/400°F/gas 6. Brush the brioche with beaten egg yolk, then bake for about 30 minutes, or until risen and golden. Turn out and cool on a wire rack. Serve warm or cold.

Pictured on page 114

BATH BUNS

PREPARATION TIME 15 minutes, plus mixing & kneading time in bread machine, plus rising
COOKING TIME 20 minutes
MAKES about 16 buns

150ml/5fl oz/⅔ cup milk (at room temperature)
2 eggs, lightly beaten
55g/2oz/4 tbsp butter, melted
500g/1lb 2oz/3½ cups strong white flour
1 tsp salt
55g/2oz/¼ cup caster/superfine sugar
2 tsp fast-action dried yeast/instant dry yeast
175g/6oz/1 cup sultanas/golden raisins
55g/2oz/⅓ cup chopped mixed candied peel
beaten egg, for glazing
25g/1oz/4 tbsp coarsely crushed sugar cubes

Whisk the milk, eggs and melted butter together in a bowl, then pour into the bread pan. Sprinkle over the flour, covering the liquid completely. Place the salt and caster/superfine sugar in separate corners of the pan. Make a small indent in the centre of the flour and add the yeast. Close the lid, set the machine to "Basic Raisin Dough" (or equivalent), or "Dough", and press Start.

Add the sultanas/golden raisins and mixed peel when the machine makes a sound (beeps) to add extra ingredients during the kneading cycle (or add 5 minutes before the end of the kneading cycle). Meanwhile, grease two baking sheets and set aside.

When the dough is ready, remove it from the machine, knock it back on a lightly floured surface, then divide the dough into about 16 equal portions. Knead each portion of the dough into a ball and place on the baking sheets. Flatten each ball slightly. Cover and leave to rise in a warm place until doubled in size.

Preheat the oven to 190°C/375°F/gas 5. Brush the tops of the buns with beaten egg and sprinkle with the crushed sugar cubes. Bake for about 20 minutes, or until risen and golden brown. Transfer to a wire rack to cool, then serve warm or cold on their own or split and spread with butter.

LARDY CAKE

PREPARATION TIME 25 minutes, plus mixing & kneading time in bread machine, plus rising

COOKING TIME 30 minutes

MAKES 1 cake (serves 10–12)

150g/5½oz/⅔ cup lard

300ml/10½ fl oz/1¼ cups water

450g/1lb/3¼ cups strong white flour

1 tsp salt

25g/1oz/2 tbsp caster/superfine sugar,
   plus 1 tbsp for the glaze

1½ tsp fast-action dried yeast/instant dry yeast

115g/4oz/½ cup packed soft light brown sugar

85g/3oz/½ cup currants

85g/3oz/½ cup sultanas/golden raisins

55g/2oz/⅓ cup chopped mixed candied peel

1 tsp ground mixed spice/apple pie spice

1 tbsp boiling water

Dice 15g/½oz/1 tablespoon of the lard. Pour the water into the bread pan. Sprinkle over the flour, covering the water completely. Place the salt, caster/superfine sugar and diced lard in separate corners of the pan. Make a small indent in the centre of the flour and add the yeast. Close the lid, set the machine to "Dough" and press Start. Meanwhile, grease a 25 x 20cm/10 x 8in shallow roasting pan and set aside.

When the dough is ready, remove it from the machine, knock it back on a floured surface, then roll out the dough to form a rectangle about 5mm/¼in thick. With a short side of the rectangle

nearest to you, dot the top two-thirds of the dough with flakes of one-third of the remaining lard. Sprinkle over one-third each of the brown sugar, dried fruits, mixed peel and spice. Fold the bottom third of the dough up over the middle third, then fold the top third down over the middle third to form a parcel. Seal the edges with a rolling pin. Give the dough a quarter turn so the folded side is to the left.

Repeat this whole procedure, rolling, filling and folding the dough, twice more, using the remaining lard, brown sugar, dried fruits, mixed peel and spice. Fold, seal and turn as before. Roll out the dough to fit the tin and place it inside. Cover and leave to rise in a warm place for about 1–1½ hours, or until almost doubled in size.

Preheat the oven to 200°C/400°F/gas 6. Score the top of the dough in a criss-cross pattern, then bake for about 30 minutes, or until risen and golden brown.

Dissolve the remaining 1 tbsp caster/superfine sugar in the boiling water, then brush this glaze over the top of the warm cake. Leave to cool in the tin for a few minutes, then turn out and serve warm or cold, cut into slices or squares.

PANETTONE

PREPARATION TIME 25 minutes, plus mixing & kneading time in bread machine, plus rising
COOKING TIME 45–50 minutes
MAKES 1 loaf (serves 8–10)

3 large eggs, lightly beaten
3 tbsp milk
375g/13oz/2⅔ cups strong white flour
½ tsp salt
55g/2oz/¼ cup caster/superfine sugar
115g/4oz/½ cup butter, softened
2 tsp fast-action dried yeast/instant dry yeast
115g/4oz/⅔ cup sultanas/golden raisins
55g/2oz/⅓ cup chopped mixed candied peel
finely grated zest of 1 small lemon
15g/½oz/1 tbsp butter, melted, for glazing

Whisk the eggs and milk in a bowl. Pour the mixture into the bread pan. Sprinkle over the flour, covering the liquid completely. Place the salt and sugar in separate corners of the pan. Dot the butter over the surface, then make a small indent in the centre of the flour and add the yeast. Close the lid, set the machine to "Basic Raisin Dough" (or equivalent), or "Dough", and press Start.

Add the sultanas/golden raisins, mixed peel and lemon zest when the machine makes a sound (beeps) to add extra ingredients during the kneading cycle (or add 5 minutes before the end of the kneading cycle).

Grease and line a deep 18cm/7in round cake tin. Tie a double layer of greaseproof paper around the outside of the tin, with string, making the collar about 7.5cm/3in above the rim. Set aside.

When the dough is ready, remove it from the machine, knock it back on a lightly floured surface, then shape the dough into a round. Place in the tin and cut a cross in the top. Cover and leave to rise in a warm place until doubled in size.

Preheat the oven to 200°C/400°F/gas 6. Brush the top of the dough with the melted butter. Bake for 15 minutes, then reduce the oven temperature to 180°C/350°F/gas 4 and bake for a further 30–35 minutes, or until the top is golden brown and crisp. Turn out and cool on a wire rack. Cut into wedges to serve.

HOT CROSS BUNS

PREPARATION TIME 20 minutes, plus mixing & kneading time in bread machine, plus rising

COOKING TIME 15–20 minutes

MAKES 12–14 buns

250ml/9fl oz/1 cup milk (at room temperature)

1 large egg, lightly beaten

450g/1lb/3¼ cups strong white flour

1 tsp ground mixed spice/apple pie spice

1 tsp ground cinnamon

1 tsp grated nutmeg

1 tsp salt

2 tbsp caster/superfine sugar

55g/2oz/4 tbsp butter, diced

1½ tsp fast-action dried yeast/instant dry yeast

finely grated zest of 1 lemon

85g/3oz/½ cup sultanas/golden raisins

25g/1oz/2 tbsp chopped mixed candied peel

85g/3oz ready-made shortcrust pastry

55g/2oz/¼ cup granulated sugar

Pour the milk into a bowl, add the egg and whisk well. Pour the mixture into the bread pan. Sprinkle over the flour, covering the liquid completely, then sprinkle over the ground spices. Place the salt, caster/superfine sugar and butter in separate corners of the pan. Make a small indent in the centre of the flour and add the yeast. Close the lid, set the machine to "Basic Raisin Dough" (or equivalent), or "Dough", and press Start.

Add the lemon zest, sultanas/golden raisins and mixed peel when the machine makes a sound (beeps) to add extra ingredients during the kneading cycle (or add 5 minutes before the end of the kneading cycle). Meanwhile, grease two baking sheets and set aside.

When the dough is ready, remove it from the machine, knock it back on a lightly floured surface, then divide the dough into 12 or 14 equal portions.

Knead each portion of dough into a ball and place on the baking sheets. Flatten each ball slightly. Roll out the pastry on a lightly floured surface and cut into narrow strips. Brush the buns with a little water and top each one with a pastry cross. Cover and leave to rise in a warm place until doubled in size.

Preheat the oven to 190°C/375°F/gas 5. Bake the buns for about 15–20 minutes, or until golden. Transfer to a wire rack.

Meanwhile, make the sugar glaze. Dissolve the granulated sugar in a saucepan with 3 tablespoons water. Heat gently, stirring until the sugar has dissolved, then bring to the boil and boil rapidly for 2 minutes. As soon as the buns come out of the oven, brush them twice with the sugar glaze. Leave to cool on a wire rack and serve warm or cold.

CROISSANTS

PREPARATION TIME 35 minutes, plus mixing & kneading time in bread machine, plus rising

COOKING TIME 15–20 minutes

MAKES 12 croissants

280g/10oz/1¼ cups butter (at room temperature)

300ml/10½ fl oz/1¼ cups milk (at room temperature)

500g/1lb 2oz/3½ cups strong white flour

1 tsp salt

2 tbsp caster/superfine sugar

1 sachet (7g/¼oz) fast-action dried yeast/ instant dry yeast

beaten egg, for glazing

Dice 55g/2oz/4 tablespoons of the butter. Pour the milk into the bread pan. Sprinkle over the flour, covering the milk completely. Place the salt, sugar and diced butter in separate corners of the pan. Make a small indent in the centre of the flour and add the yeast. Close the lid, set the machine to "Dough" and press Start.

Meanwhile, grease two baking sheets and set aside. When the dough is ready, remove it from the machine, knock it back on a lightly floured surface, then roll out the dough to form a rectangle measuring about 35 x 18cm/14 x 7in.

Flatten the remaining butter into a block about 2cm/¾in thick. With a short side of the dough rectangle nearest to you, place the butter on top of the dough so that it covers the top two-thirds of the rectangle. Fold the bottom third of the dough over the middle third, then fold the top buttered third down over the top of the middle third to form a parcel. Seal the edges with a rolling pin.

Give the dough a quarter turn so the folded side is to the left. Roll into a rectangle as before, then fold the bottom third up and the top third down and seal the edges, as before. Wrap in greaseproof/wax paper and chill in the refrigerator for 20 minutes. Repeat the rolling, folding and chilling twice more, turning the dough 90 degrees each time before rolling.

Roll out the dough on a lightly floured surface to form a 53 x 35cm/21 x 14in rectangle and cut into 12 equal triangles. Roll each triangle into a sausage shape, starting from the long side and ending with the point of the triangle. Bend the ends of each croissant round to make a crescent or half-moon shape. Place on the baking sheets. Cover and leave to rise in a warm place for about 30 minutes, or until almost doubled in size.

Preheat the oven to 220°C/425°F/gas 7. Lightly brush the croissants with beaten egg, then bake for 15–20 minutes, or until crisp and golden brown. Transfer to a wire rack to cool. Serve warm.

CHELSEA BUNS

PREPARATION TIME 20 minutes, plus mixing & kneading time in bread machine, plus rising
COOKING TIME 25–30 minutes
MAKES 12 buns

100ml/3½fl oz/scant ½ cup tbsp milk (at room temperature)

1 large egg, lightly beaten

225g/8oz/1⅔ cups strong white flour

½ tsp salt

2 tbsp caster/superfine sugar

55g/2oz/4 tbsp butter, diced

1 tsp fast-action dried yeast/instant dry yeast

85g/3oz/½ cup mixed raisins and currants

55g/2oz/⅓ cup sultanas/golden raisins

55g/2oz/¼ cup packed soft light brown sugar

1½ tsp ground cinnamon

2 tbsp clear honey, for glazing

Whisk the milk and egg together in a bowl and pour into the bread pan. Sprinkle over the flour, covering the liquid completely. Place the salt, caster/superfine sugar and 25g/1oz/2 tbsp of the butter in separate corners of the pan. Make a small indent in the centre of the flour and add the yeast. Close the lid, set the machine to "Dough" and press Start.

Grease an 18cm/7in square cake tin and set aside. When the dough is ready, remove it from the machine, knock it back on a lightly floured surface, then roll it out into a rectangle measuring 30 x 23cm/12 x 9in.

Melt the remaining butter and brush it over the dough. Combine the dried fruit, brown sugar and cinnamon and sprinkle evenly over the dough, leaving a 2.5cm/1in border around the edges.

Starting from a long side, roll up the dough fairly tightly like a Swiss roll. Cut into 12 even slices and place, cut side up, in the tin. Cover and leave to rise in a warm place until doubled in size.

Preheat the oven to 190°C/375°F/gas 5. Bake the buns for about 25–30 minutes, or until risen and golden brown. Remove from the oven and brush twice with honey while still hot. Cool slightly, then turn out onto a wire rack. Serve warm or cold.

EASTER BREAD RING

PREPARATION TIME 25 minutes, plus mixing & kneading time in bread machine, plus rising
COOKING TIME 20–25 minutes
MAKES 1 ring (serves 10–12)

100ml/3½fl oz/scant ½ cup milk (at room temperature), plus extra for glazing

1 large egg, lightly beaten

225g/8oz/1⅔ cups strong white flour

½ tsp salt

2 tbsp caster/superfine sugar

55g/2oz/4 tbsp butter, diced

1 tsp fast-action dried yeast/instant dry yeast

85g/3oz/½ cup sultanas/golden raisins

85g/3oz/½ cup ready-to-eat dried apricots, chopped

55g/2oz/¼ cup packed soft light brown sugar

1½ tsp ground mixed spice/apple pie spice

115g/4oz/scant 1 cup icing/confectioners' sugar, sifted

25g/1oz/¼ cup toasted flaked/sliced almonds

Whisk the milk and egg together in a bowl and pour into the bread pan. Sprinkle over the flour, covering the liquid completely. Place the salt, caster/superfine sugar and 25g/1oz/2 tbsp of the butter in separate corners of the pan. Make a small indent in the centre of the flour and add the yeast. Close the lid, set the machine to "Dough" and press Start.

Grease a baking sheet and set aside. When the dough is ready, remove it from the machine, knock it back on a lightly floured surface, then roll it out into a 46 x 30cm/18 x 12in rectangle. Melt the remaining butter and brush it over the dough. Sprinkle evenly with the dried fruit, brown sugar and spice.

Starting from a long side, roll up the dough like a Swiss roll, then shape it into a circle, seam-side down. Brush the ends with milk and press them together to seal. Place the dough ring on the baking sheet.

Using a sharp knife, make cuts two-thirds of the way through the dough at 4cm/1½in intervals, twisting the slices outwards at an angle so they overlap slightly. Cover and leave to rise in a warm place until doubled in size.

Preheat the oven to 200°C/400°F/gas 6. Bake the bread ring for 20–25 minutes, or until golden brown. Transfer to a wire rack to cool.

Mix the icing/confectioners' sugar with about 4 teaspoons water in a small bowl to make a thin glacé icing and drizzle it over the warm baked ring. Sprinkle with the almonds. Serve warm or cold in slices.

DOUGHNUTS

PREPARATION TIME 20 minutes, plus mixing & kneading time in bread machine, plus rising

COOKING TIME 25 minutes

MAKES 16 doughnuts

175ml/6fl oz/¾ cup milk (at room temperature)

2 large eggs, lightly beaten

500g/1lb 2oz/3½ cups strong white flour

1 tsp salt

175g/6oz/¾ cup plus 2 tbsp caster/superfine sugar

25g/1oz/2 tbsp butter, diced

1½ tsp fast-action dried yeast/instant dry yeast

115g/4oz/⅓ cup strawberry or raspberry jam

sunflower oil, for deep-frying

1½ tsp ground cinnamon

Pour the milk into a bowl, add the eggs and whisk well. Pour the mixture into the bread pan. Sprinkle over the flour, covering the liquid completely. Place the salt, 85g/3oz/7 tbsp of the sugar and the butter in separate corners of the pan. Make a small indent in the centre of the flour and add the yeast. Close the lid, set the machine to "Dough" and press Start.

Meanwhile, oil two baking sheets and set aside. When the dough is ready, remove it from the machine, knock it back on a lightly floured surface, then divide the dough into 16 equal portions.

Shape each portion of the dough into a ball, then flatten each one into a disc about 1cm/½in thick. Place 1 heaped teaspoon of jam into the middle of each disc, gather the edges of the dough up and over the jam, enclosing it completely, then pinch the edges firmly together to seal, and roll into a ball. Place on the baking sheets, cover and leave to rise in a warm place for about 30 minutes, or until almost doubled in size.

Heat some oil in a deep-fat fryer to 170°C/325°F and then fry the doughnuts in batches in the hot oil for about 6 minutes, or until golden all over, turning once. Remove the doughnuts from the fryer using a slotted spoon and drain on paper towels.

Combine the remaining sugar and the cinnamon in a bowl. Toss the warm doughnuts in the sugar mixture, coating them all over. Serve immediately.

PAINS AU CHOCOLAT

PREPARATION TIME 35 minutes, plus mixing & kneading time in bread machine, plus rising

COOKING TIME 15–20 minutes

MAKES 12 pains au chocolat

280g/10oz/1¼ cups butter (at room temperature)

300ml/10½ fl oz/1¼ cups milk (at room temperature)

500g/1lb 2oz/3½ cups strong white flour

1 tsp salt

2 tbsp caster/superfine sugar

1 sachet (7g/¼oz) fast-action dried yeast/ instant dry yeast

175g/6oz plain/semisweet or milk chocolate, finely chopped

beaten egg, for glazing

Dice 55g/2oz/4 tablespoons of the butter. Pour the milk into the bread pan. Sprinkle over the flour, covering the milk completely. Place the salt, sugar and diced butter in separate corners of the pan. Make a small indent in the centre of the flour and add the yeast. Close the lid, set the machine to "Dough" and press Start.

Grease two baking sheets and set aside. When the dough is ready, remove it from the machine, knock it back on a lightly floured surface, then roll out the dough to form a rectangle about 53 x 35cm/21 x 14in.

Flatten the remaining butter into a block about 2cm/¾in thick. With a short side of the dough rectangle nearest to you, place the butter on top of the dough so that it covers the top two-thirds

of the rectangle. Fold the bottom third of the dough over the middle third, then fold the top buttered third down over the top of the middle third to form a parcel. Seal the edges with a rolling pin.

Give the dough a quarter turn so the folded side is to the left. Roll into a rectangle as before, then fold the bottom third up and the top third down and seal the edges, as before. Wrap in greaseproof/ wax paper and chill in the refrigerator for about 20 minutes. Repeat the rolling, folding and chilling twice more, turning the dough 90 degrees each time, before rolling.

Roll out the dough on a lightly floured surface to form a 53 x 35cm/21 x 14in rectangle and cut into 12 equal rectangles. Place 15g/½oz of the chopped chocolate at one end of each rectangle. Roll up each rectangle to make a flattish cylinder shape, enclosing the chocolate completely. Place seam-side down on the baking sheets. Cover and leave to rise in a warm place until almost doubled in size.

Preheat the oven to 200°C/400°F/gas 6. Lightly brush the pastries with beaten egg, then bake for 15–20 minutes, or until crisp and golden brown. Transfer to a wire rack to cool. Serve warm.

DANISH APPLE PLAIT

PREPARATION TIME 25 minutes, plus mixing & kneading time in bread machine, plus rising

COOKING TIME 20–25 minutes

MAKES 1 loaf (serves 8)

100ml/3½fl oz/scant ½ cup milk
   (at room temperature)

1 large egg, lightly beaten

250g/9oz/1¾ cups strong white flour

½ tsp salt

25g/1oz/2 tbsp butter, diced

55g/2oz/¼ cup caster/superfine sugar

1 tsp fast-action dried yeast/instant dry yeast

140g/5oz ready-made marzipan or almond
   paste, coarsely grated

1 large or 2 small cooking apples, peeled, cored
   and thinly sliced

1 tsp ground cinnamon

beaten egg, for glazing

85g/3oz/¾ cup icing/confectioners' sugar, sifted

15g/½oz/1 tbsp toasted flaked/sliced almonds
   or chopped pistachio nuts, to decorate

Whisk the milk and egg together in a bowl and pour into the bread pan. Sprinkle over the flour, covering the liquid completely. Place the salt, butter and 25g/1oz/2 tbsp of the caster/ superfine sugar in separate corners of the pan. Make a small indent in the centre of the flour and add the yeast. Close the lid, set the machine to "Dough" and press Start.

Grease a baking sheet and set aside. When the dough is ready, remove it from the machine, knock it back on a lightly floured surface, then roll it out to form a 30 x 25cm/12 x 10in rectangle. Place the marzipan evenly down the centre third (lengthways) of the dough (about 6–7.5cm/ 2½–3in wide).

Toss the apple slices with the remaining caster/ superfine sugar and the cinnamon, then spoon this mixture evenly over the marzipan. On the longest sides of the dough, make diagonal cuts up to the filling at 2.5cm/1in intervals. Plait the strips of dough over the filling, pressing lightly to seal. Tuck the ends under to seal at both ends of the plait. Place the plait on the baking sheet, then cover and leave to rise in a warm place until doubled in size.

Preheat the oven to 200°C/400°F/gas 6. Lightly brush the plait with beaten egg, then bake for about 20–25 minutes, or until risen and golden. Transfer to a wire rack to cool.

Combine the icing/confectioners' sugar with a little water in a small bowl to make a thin glacé icing. Drizzle the icing over the warm plait, then sprinkle with the almonds or pistachios. Serve warm or cold in slices.

STOLLEN

PREPARATION TIME 25 minutes, plus mixing & kneading time in bread machine, plus rising
COOKING TIME 40 minutes
MAKES 1 loaf (serves 10–12)

150ml/5fl oz/⅔ cup milk (at room temperature)

1 large egg, lightly beaten

350g/12oz/2⅔ cups strong white flour

1 tsp ground mixed spice/apple pie spice

½ tsp salt

2 tbsp caster/superfine sugar

40g/1½oz/3 tbsp butter, diced

1½ tsp fast-action dried yeast/instant dry yeast

175g/6oz/1 cup luxury mixed dried fruit

55g/2oz/½ cup blanched almonds, finely chopped

finely grated zest of 1 lemon

175g/6oz ready-made marzipan or almond paste

icing/confectioners' sugar and ground cinnamon, for dusting

Whisk the milk and egg together in a bowl and pour into the bread pan. Sprinkle over the flour, covering the liquid completely, then sprinkle over the spice. Place the salt, caster/superfine sugar and butter in separate corners of the pan. Make a small indent in the centre of the flour and add the yeast. Close the lid, set the machine to "Basic Raisin Dough" (or equivalent), or "Dough", and press Start.

Mix together the dried fruit, almonds and lemon zest and set aside. Add the dried fruit mixture when the machine makes a sound (beeps) to add extra ingredients during the kneading cycle (or add 5 minutes before the end of the kneading cycle).

Grease a baking sheet and set aside. When the dough is ready, remove it from the machine, knock it back on a lightly floured surface, then roll it out into a rectangle measuring 23 x 15cm/9 x 6in.

Roll the marzipan into a long sausage shape, just a little shorter than the length of the rectangle, and place the marzipan log along the centre of the dough. Fold the dough over almost in half to enclose it and press the edges together to seal. Transfer to the baking sheet, cover and leave to rise in a warm place until doubled in size.

Preheat the oven to 180°C/350°F/gas 4. Bake the loaf for about 40 minutes, or until deep golden brown. Transfer to a wire rack to cool. Dust with a mixture of sifted icing/confectioners' sugar and cinnamon. Serve in slices.

APPLE & CINNAMON PULL-APART

PREPARATION TIME 25 minutes, plus mixing & kneading time in bread machine, plus rising

COOKING TIME 25–30 minutes

MAKES 1 loaf (serves 12)

150ml/5fl oz/²⁄₃ cup milk (at room temperature)

125ml/4fl oz/½ cup water

1 large egg, lightly beaten

450g/1lb/3¼ cups strong white flour

1 tsp salt

2 tbsp caster/superfine sugar

2 tsp fast-action dried yeast/instant dry yeast

175g/6oz/¾ cup packed light soft
   brown sugar

1½ tsp ground cinnamon

3 eating apples, peeled, cored and thinly sliced

4 tbsp double/heavy cream

25g/1oz/2 tbsp butter, diced

25g/1oz/¼ cup hazelnuts, finely chopped

Whisk the milk, water and egg together in a bowl and pour into the bread pan. Sprinkle over the flour, covering the liquid completely. Place the salt and caster/superfine sugar in separate corners of the pan. Make a small indent in the centre of the flour and add the yeast. Close the lid, set the machine to "Dough" and press Start.

Grease a 23cm/9in loose-bottomed springform tin fitted with a tube base, or a ring mould, and set aside. When the dough is ready, remove it from the machine, knock it back on a lightly floured surface, then roll out the dough to form a 40 x 20cm/16 x 8in rectangle.

Combine 55g/2oz/¼ cup of the brown sugar and the cinnamon, then add the apple slices and toss to mix well. Spoon the mixture evenly over the dough, leaving a 1cm/½in border around the edges. Starting from a long side, roll up the dough fairly tightly like a Swiss roll. Cut into 12 even slices, then place the slices upright but at an angle (so they rest on each other) in the tin. Cover and leave to rise in a warm place for about 1½–2 hours, or until doubled in size.

Preheat the oven to 190°C/375°F/gas 5. Bake for 25–30 minutes, or until risen and golden brown. Cool slightly in the tin, then turn out onto a wire rack.

Meanwhile, place the remaining brown sugar, the cream and butter in a small pan and heat gently, stirring, until the sugar has dissolved. Bring gently to the boil, then simmer, uncovered, for about 4 minutes, or until the mixture thickens slightly.

Brush the hot pull-apart with the caramel mixture, then sprinkle with the hazelnuts. Pull the rolls apart to serve and serve warm or cold.

TEABREADS &
TEA-TIME TREATS

Delicious, moist teabreads are perfect for serving with a cup of tea
or coffee as a tasty afternoon snack, although most can be enjoyed
as a treat at any time of the day.

Teabreads are generally easy to make and those that are enriched with
butter or eggs will keep well for a few days if wrapped or stored in an
airtight container. Other treats, such as teacakes and muffins,
should be eaten freshly baked or toasted.

Choose from iced delights such as Lemon Blueberry Loaf and Iced
Orange Teabread, or enjoy munching on Marbled Chocolate Teabread
or Hawaiian Fruit Teabread. For a more traditional and hard-to-resist
tea-time treat, split and toast some Teacake Fingers and serve them hot,
spread with melting butter.

MARBLED CHOCOLATE TEABREAD

PREPARATION TIME 25 minutes

COOKING TIME 55–65 minutes

MAKES 1 loaf (serves 10)

175g/6oz/¾ cup butter, softened

175g/6oz/¾ cup packed soft light brown sugar

3 eggs, beaten

225g/8oz/1⅔ cups plain/
all-purpose white flour

2½ tsp baking powder

2 ripe bananas, peeled and mashed with
a little lemon juice

25g/1oz/¼ cup cocoa powder

2 tsp milk

½ tsp ground ginger

sifted icing/confectioners' sugar and cocoa
powder, for dusting (optional)

Remove the kneading blade from the bread pan. Remove the bread pan from the machine, grease and line the base and sides of the pan and set aside.

Cream the butter and brown sugar together in a bowl. Gradually beat in the eggs. Sift over the flour and baking powder and fold in, mixing well. Fold in the mashed bananas.

Place half the mixture in a separate bowl; sift over the cocoa powder, add the milk and fold together. Stir the ground ginger into the plain banana mixture. Place alternate spoonfuls of each mixture into the bread pan, then gently swirl a sharp knife or skewer through the mixture to create a marbled effect.

Place the bread pan in position in the machine and close the lid. Set the machine to "Bake Only" for 55 minutes. Press Start.

After baking, a fine skewer inserted in the centre of the teabread should come out clean. If the teabread requires further baking, bake on the same setting for a further 5–10 minutes, or until cooked.

Remove the bread pan from the machine and leave to stand for 10 minutes, then turn the teabread out onto a wire rack to cool. Dust with icing/confectioners' sugar and cocoa powder, if desired, and serve warm or cold in slices.

MALTED SULTANA LOAF

PREPARATION TIME 10 minutes
COOKING TIME varies according to bread machine
MAKES 1 loaf (serves 10)

350ml/12fl oz/1½ cups water
3 tbsp malt extract
500g/1lb 2oz/3½ cups strong white flour
1 tbsp skimmed milk powder
1½ tsp salt
2 tsp caster/superfine sugar
25g/1oz/2 tbsp butter, diced
1 tsp fast-action dried yeast/instant dry yeast
115g/4oz/⅔ cup sultanas/golden raisins

Pour the water into the bread pan, then add the malt extract. Sprinkle over the flour, covering the liquid completely. Sprinkle the milk powder over the flour. Place the salt, sugar and butter in separate corners of the pan. Make a small indent in the centre of the flour and add the yeast.

Close the lid, set the machine to "Basic White"/ "Normal", with "Raisin", if available (or equivalent), then select the loaf size and crust type. Press Start.

Add the sultanas/golden raisins when the machine makes a sound (beeps) to add extra ingredients during the kneading cycle (or add 5 minutes before the end of the kneading cycle).

After baking, remove the bread pan from the machine, then turn the loaf out onto a wire rack to cool. Serve in slices.

VARIATION Use raisins, sweetened dried cranberries or chopped ready-to-eat dried apricots or pears in place of the sultanas/golden raisins.

BANANA-CHIP MUESLI TEABREAD

PREPARATION TIME 15 minutes

COOKING TIME 1–1¼ hours

MAKES 1 loaf (serves 10)

175g/6oz/¾ cup butter, softened

175g/6oz/¾ cup packed soft light brown sugar

3 eggs, beaten

175g/6oz/1⅓ cups self-raising/
self-rising white flour

55g/2oz/½ cup muesli (of your choice), such as
Swiss-style muesli

85g/3oz/½ cup banana chips

sifted icing/confectioners' sugar, to decorate
(optional)

Remove the kneading blade from the bread pan. Remove the bread pan from the machine, grease and line the base and sides of the pan and set aside.

Cream the butter and brown sugar together in a bowl until light and fluffy, then gradually beat in the eggs. Sift the flour into the bowl, then fold the flour into the creamed mixture together with the muesli and banana chips, mixing well. Spoon the mixture into the bread pan and level the surface.

Place the bread pan in position in the machine and close the lid. Set the machine to "Bake Only" for 60 minutes. Press Start.

After baking, a fine skewer inserted in the centre of the teabread should come out clean. If the teabread requires further baking, bake on the same setting for a further 10–15 minutes, or until cooked.

Remove the bread pan from the machine using oven gloves, then leave to stand for 10 minutes, before turning the teabread out onto a wire rack to cool. Dust with sifted icing/confectioners' sugar, if desired, and serve warm or cold in slices.

ICED ORANGE TEABREAD

PREPARATION TIME 15 minutes

COOKING TIME 1 hour–1 hour 10 minutes

MAKES 1 loaf (serves 10)

FOR THE TEABREAD

115g/4oz/½ cup butter, softened

55g/2oz/¼ cup packed soft light brown sugar

2 eggs, beaten

140g/5oz/1 cup self-raising/self-rising
  white flour, sifted

140g/5oz/1 cup self-raising/self-rising
  wholemeal/wholewheat flour

1½ tsp ground ginger

8 tbsp orange marmalade (about 200g/7oz)

about 1 tbsp milk

FOR THE ICING

85g/3oz/6 tbsp butter, softened

1 tsp finely grated orange zest

175g/6oz/1½ cups icing/confectioners' sugar,
  sifted

2 tsp orange juice

thinly pared orange zest, to decorate (optional)

Remove the kneading blade from the bread pan. Remove the bread pan from the machine, grease and line the base and sides of the pan and set aside.

For the teabread, cream the butter and brown sugar together in a bowl until light and fluffy, then gradually beat in the eggs. Fold the flours and ground ginger into the creamed mixture, mixing well. Fold in the marmalade and enough milk to make a fairly soft consistency. Spoon the mixture into the bread pan and level the surface.

Place the bread pan in position in the machine and close the lid. Set the machine to "Bake Only" for 60 minutes. Press Start.

After baking, a fine skewer inserted in the centre of the teabread should come out clean. If the teabread requires further baking, bake on the same setting for a further 5–10 minutes, or until cooked.

Remove the bread pan from the machine using oven gloves. Leave to stand for 10 minutes, before turning the teabread out onto a wire rack to cool.

Meanwhile, make the icing. Cream the butter in a bowl until pale and fluffy, then beat in the orange zest. Gradually stir in the icing/confectioners' sugar and orange juice, mixing to make a soft icing. Spread the icing over the top of the cold teabread and sprinkle with the pared orange zest, if desired. Serve in slices.

LEMON BLUEBERRY LOAF

PREPARATION TIME 15 minutes

COOKING TIME 1–1¼ hours

MAKES 1 loaf (serves 10)

225g/8oz/1⅔ cups self-raising/
self-rising white flour

115g/4oz/½ cup butter, diced

115g/4oz/½ cup plus 1 tbsp caster/
superfine sugar

40g/1½oz/⅓ cup ground almonds or hazelnuts

finely grated zest and juice of 1 lemon

2 eggs, beaten

4 tbsp milk

200g/7oz/1½ cups fresh blueberries,
rinsed and dried

55g/2oz/½ cup icing/confectioners' sugar, sifted

Remove the kneading blade from the bread pan. Remove the bread pan from the machine, grease and line the base and sides of the pan and set aside.

Sift the flour into a bowl, then lightly rub in the butter. Stir in the caster/superfine sugar, nuts and lemon zest, then beat in the eggs and milk, mixing well. Fold in the blueberries. Spoon the mixture into the bread pan and level the surface.

Place the bread pan in position in the machine and close the lid. Set the machine to "Bake Only" for 60 minutes. Press Start.

After baking, a fine skewer inserted in the centre of the loaf should come out clean. If the loaf requires further baking, bake on the same setting for a further 10–15 minutes, or until cooked.

Remove the pan from the machine using oven gloves. Leave to stand for 10 minutes, before turning the loaf out onto a wire rack to cool completely.

Meanwhile, make the icing. Combine the icing/confectioners' sugar with 1–2 teaspoons lemon juice in a small bowl to make a fairly thin glacé icing. Drizzle the icing over the cold loaf. Serve in slices.

ICED RAISIN LOAF

PREPARATION TIME 20 minutes, plus overnight soaking

COOKING TIME 1¼ hours–1 hour 25 minutes

MAKES 1 loaf (serves 10–12)

225g/8oz/1¼ cups raisins

115g/4oz/⅔ cup sultanas/golden raisins

300ml/10½fl oz/1¼ cups strong hot tea, strained

225g/8oz/1¼ cups packed soft light brown sugar

300g/10½oz/2 cups plus 2 tbsp self-raising/self-rising white flour

1½ tsp ground mixed spice/apple pie spice

1 egg, beaten

175g /6oz/1½ cups icing/confectioners' sugar, sifted

about 5–6 tsp orange juice

Place the raisins and sultanas/golden raisins in a large bowl, pour over the hot tea and stir to mix. Cover and leave to soak overnight.

The next day, remove the kneading blade from the bread pan. Remove the bread pan from the machine, grease and line the base and sides of the pan and set aside. Stir the brown sugar into the fruit mixture, then sift in the flour and spice.

Add the egg and mix throroughly with a wooden spoon. Spoon the mixture into the bread pan and level the surface.

Place the bread pan in position in the machine and close the lid. Set the machine to "Bake Only" for 75 minutes. Press Start.

After baking, a fine skewer inserted in the centre of the loaf should come out clean. If not, bake on the same setting for a further 5–10 minutes, or until cooked.

Remove the bread pan from the machine using oven gloves, then leave to stand for 5 minutes, before turning the loaf out onto a wire rack to cool completely.

Combine the icing/confectioners' sugar with enough orange juice in a bowl to make a thick, smooth icing. Spread the icing evenly over the top of the cold loaf. Leave to set. Serve in slices.

Pictured on page 140

APRICOT & WALNUT TEABREAD

PREPARATION TIME 20 minutes

COOKING TIME 1–1¼ hours

MAKES 1 loaf (serves 10)

280g/10oz/2 cups plain/all-purpose white flour

2½ tsp baking powder

1½ tsp ground mixed spice/apple pie spice

85g/3oz/6 tbsp butter, diced

85g/3oz/½ cup packed soft light brown sugar

200g/7oz/1¼ cups ready-to-eat dried apricots, chopped

115g/4oz/⅔ cup sultanas/golden raisins

85g/3oz/⅔ cup walnuts, chopped

200ml/7fl oz/scant 1 cup milk

1 egg, beaten

Remove the kneading blade from the bread pan. Remove the bread pan from the machine, grease and line the base and sides of the pan and set aside.

Sift the flour, baking powder and spice into a bowl, then lightly rub in the butter. Stir in the sugar, apricots, sultanas/golden raisins and walnuts. Gradually beat in the milk and egg until well mixed. Spoon the mixture into the bread pan and level the surface.

Place the bread pan in position in the machine and close the lid. Set the machine to "Bake Only" for 60 minutes. Press Start.

After baking, a fine skewer inserted in the centre of the teabread should come out clean. If the teabread requires further baking, bake on the same setting for a further 10–15 minutes, or until cooked.

Remove the bread pan from the machine using oven gloves, then leave to stand for 5 minutes, before turning the teabread out onto a wire rack to cool. Serve warm or cold in slices.

VARIATIONS Use raisins or dried blueberries in place of the sultanas/golden raisins. Use hazelnuts or pecans in place of the walnuts.

HAWAIIAN FRUIT TEABREAD

PREPARATION TIME 15 minutes, plus overnight soaking

COOKING TIME 1–1¼ hours

MAKES 1 loaf (serves 10)

225g/8oz/1¼ cups mixed ready-to-eat dried tropical fruit, chopped

175ml/6fl oz/¾ cup strong hot tea, strained

225g/8oz/1⅔ cups plain/all-purpose wholemeal/wholewheat flour

1 tbsp baking powder

1½ tsp ground mixed spice/apple pie spice

175g/6oz/¾ cup packed soft light brown sugar

finely grated zest of 1 orange

25g/1oz/¼ cup desiccated/dried shredded coconut

1 egg, beaten

4 tbsp milk

sifted icing/confectioners' sugar, to decorate

Put the mixed fruit into a large bowl, pour over the hot tea, stir to mix, then leave to soak overnight.

The next day, remove the kneading blade from the bread pan. Remove the bread pan from the machine, grease and line the base and sides of the pan and set aside.

Combine the flour, baking powder, spice, brown sugar, orange zest and coconut in a bowl. Add to the soaked fruits, together with the egg and milk, and mix thoroughly. Spoon into the bread pan and level the surface.

Place the bread pan in position in the machine and close the lid. Set the machine to "Bake Only" for 60 minutes. Press Start.

After baking, a fine skewer inserted in the centre of the teabread should come out clean. If the teabread requires further baking, bake on the same setting for a further 10–15 minutes, or until cooked.

Remove the bread pan from the machine using oven gloves. Leave to stand for 5 minutes, before turning the teabread out onto a wire rack to cool. Dust with sifted icing/confectioners' sugar. Serve warm or cold in slices.

TEACAKES

PREPARATION TIME 15 minutes, plus mixing & kneading time in bread machine, plus rising

COOKING TIME 20–25 minutes

MAKES 8 teacakes

300ml/10½ fl oz/1¼ cups milk (at room temperature), plus extra for glazing

450g/1lb/3¼ cups strong white flour

1¼ tsp salt

25g/1oz/2 tbsp caster/superfine sugar

25g/1oz/2 tbsp butter, diced

1½ tsp fast-action dried yeast/instant dry yeast

115g/4oz/⅔ cup currants

Pour the milk into the bread pan. Sprinkle over the flour, covering the milk completely. Place the salt, sugar and butter in separate corners of the pan. Make a small indent in the centre of the flour and add the yeast. Close the lid, set the machine to "Basic Raisin Dough" (or equivalent), or "Dough", and press Start.

Add the currants when the machine makes a sound (beeps) to add extra ingredients during the kneading cycle (or add 5 minutes before the end of the kneading cycle). Meanwhile, grease two baking sheets and set aside.

When the dough is ready, remove it from the machine, knock it back on a lightly floured surface, then divide the dough into eight equal portions. Roll and shape each portion of the dough into a round teacake and prick each one twice on top with a fork. Place on the baking sheets, cover and leave to rise in a warm place until doubled in size.

Preheat the oven to 200°C/400°F/gas 6. Brush the teacakes with a little milk, then bake for 20–25 minutes, or until risen and golden brown. Transfer to a wire rack to cool. To serve, split each teacake in half, toast lightly and then spread with butter or jam.

TEACAKE FINGERS

PREPARATION TIME 15 minutes, plus mixing & kneading time in bread machine, plus rising
COOKING TIME 20 minutes
MAKES 12 teacake fingers

150ml/5fl oz/⅔ cup milk (at room temperature)
175ml/6fl oz/¾ cup warm water
(or according to bread mix packet instructions)
500g/1lb 2oz packet white bread mix
2 tbsp caster/superfine sugar
1 tsp ground mixed spice/apple pie spice
25g/1oz/2 tbsp butter, diced
115g/4oz/⅔ cup sultanas/golden raisins
55g/2oz/⅓ cup chopped mixed candied peel
beaten egg, for glazing

Pour the milk and correct amount of water into the bread pan. Sprinkle over the bread mix, covering the liquid completely. Sprinkle over the sugar and spice, then dot the butter over the surface. Close the lid, set the machine to "Basic Raisin Dough" (or equivalent), or "Dough", and press Start.

Add the sultanas/golden raisins and mixed peel when the machine makes a sound (beeps) to add extra ingredients during the kneading cycle (or add 5 minutes before the end of the kneading cycle).

Meanwhile, grease or flour two baking sheets and set aside. When the dough is ready, remove it from the machine, knock it back on a lightly floured surface, then divide the dough into 12 equal portions.

Roll and shape each portion of the dough into a long roll or finger shape and place on the baking sheets. Cover and leave to rise in a warm place for about 30 minutes, or until doubled in size.

Preheat the oven to 190°C/375°F/gas 5. Brush the teacakes with beaten egg, then bake for about 20 minutes, or until risen and golden brown. Transfer to a wire rack to cool. Serve split, lightly toasted and spread with butter.

ENGLISH MUFFINS

PREPARATION TIME 20 minutes, plus mixing & kneading time in bread machine, plus rising
COOKING TIME 35–45 minutes
MAKES 8–10 muffins

140ml/4½fl oz/½ cup plus 1 tbsp milk (at room temperature)
125ml/4fl oz/½ cup water
55g/2oz/4 tbsp butter, melted
450g/1lb/3¼ cups strong white flour
1½ tsp salt
1 tsp caster/superfine sugar
1½ tsp fast-action dried yeast/instant dry yeast
sunflower oil, for greasing

Pour the milk and water into a bowl, add the melted butter and whisk well. Pour the mixture into the bread pan. Sprinkle over the flour, covering the liquid completely. Place the salt and sugar in separate corners of the pan. Make a small indent in the centre of the flour and add the yeast. Close the lid, set the machine to "Dough" and press Start.

Meanwhile, generously flour a large baking sheet and set aside. When the dough is ready, remove it from the machine, knock it back on a lightly floured surface, then divide the dough into 8–10 equal portions.

Shape each portion of the dough into a round with straight sides, each about 1–2 cm/½–¾in thick. Place on the baking sheet, cover and leave to rise in a warm place for about 30–40 minutes, or until springy to the touch.

Brush a griddle/grill pan or large, heavy frying pan with a little oil and heat until warm. Carefully transfer 3–4 muffins onto the griddle/grill pan and cook over a moderate heat for 8–10 minutes, or until golden brown underneath. Turn them over and cook the other side for about 8 minutes, or until golden brown.

Remove the muffins from the pan and wrap them in a clean tea towel, if serving warm. Otherwise, transfer them to a wire rack to cool. Cook the remaining muffins in the same way in batches.

To serve, split the warm muffins open and serve with butter. If serving from cold, toast the muffins on both sides, then split and spread with butter.

ENGLISH WHOLEMEAL MUFFINS

PREPARATION TIME 20 minutes, plus mixing & kneading time in bread machine, plus rising

COOKING TIME 35–45 minutes

MAKES 8–10 muffins

350ml/12fl oz/1½ cups milk (at room temperature)

225g/8oz/1⅔ cups strong white flour

225g/8oz/1⅔ cups strong wholemeal/ wholewheat flour

1½ tsp salt

1 tsp caster/superfine sugar

15g/½oz/1 tbsp butter, diced

1½ tsp fast-action dried yeast/instant dry yeast

sunflower oil, for greasing

Pour the milk into the bread pan. Sprinkle over each flour in turn, covering the milk completely. Place the salt, sugar and butter in separate corners of the pan. Make a small indent in the centre of the flour and add the yeast. Close the lid, set the machine to "Dough" and press Start.

Meanwhile, generously flour a large baking sheet and set aside. When the dough is ready, remove it from the machine, knock it back on a lightly floured surface, then divide the dough into 8–10 equal portions.

Shape each portion of the dough into a round with straight sides, about 1–2cm/½–¾in thick. Place on the baking sheet, cover and leave to rise in a warm place for about 30 minutes, or until almost doubled in size.

Brush a griddle/grill pan or large, heavy frying pan with a little oil and heat until warm. Carefully transfer 3–4 muffins onto the griddle/grill pan and cook over a moderate heat for 7–10 minutes, or until golden brown underneath. Turn them over and cook the other side for about 7 minutes, or until golden brown.

Remove the muffins from the pan and wrap them in a clean tea towel, if serving warm. Otherwise, transfer them to a wire rack to cool. Cook the remaining muffins in the same way in batches.

To serve, split the warm muffins open and serve with butter. If serving from cold, toast the muffins on both sides, then split and spread with butter.

GLUTEN-FREE BREADS

For those with a sensitivity to gluten, this chapter will be an invaluable source of creative and tasty recipes.

Gluten-free breads, by the very nature of the ingredients used to create them, tend to be slightly different in texture and flavour from ordinary breads, but are just as appealing and delicious. They have a slightly more crumbly, closer, but light texture, and many are enjoyed at their best when served warm and freshly baked.

There is an excellent selection of gluten-free recipes in this chapter, including Basic Gluten-free White Bread and Basic Gluten-free Brown Bread, Fresh Herb Bread and Italian Tomato Bread, as well as tasty sweet recipes such as Spiced Honey Loaf and Apricot & Cranberry Teabread.

BASIC GLUTEN-FREE BROWN BREAD

PREPARATION TIME 10 minutes
COOKING TIME varies according to
    bread machine
MAKES 1 loaf (serves 10–12)

325ml/11fl oz/1⅓ cups milk (at room temperature)
4 tbsp sunflower oil
2 eggs, lightly beaten
450g/1lb/3¼ cups gluten-free brown bread flour
2 tbsp caster/superfine sugar
1 tsp salt
1 sachet (7g/¼oz) fast-action dried yeast/
    instant dry yeast

Pour the milk into a bowl, add the oil and eggs
and whisk together well to mix. Pour the mixture into
the bread pan. Sprinkle over the flour, covering the
liquid completely. Sprinkle the sugar evenly over
the flour, then add the salt. Make a small indent
in the centre of the flour and add the yeast.

Close the lid, set the machine to "Rapid Bake" (or
equivalent), then select the loaf size and crust type.
Press Start.

A couple of minutes after mixing has begun, lift
the lid of the machine briefly and scrape down the
sides of the pan with a plastic spatula to ensure
even mixing. Close the lid once again.

After baking, remove the bread pan from the
machine and turn the loaf out onto a wire rack
to cool. Serve in slices.

BASIC GLUTEN-FREE WHITE BREAD

PREPARATION TIME 10 minutes
COOKING TIME varies according to
    bread machine
MAKES 1 loaf (serves 10–12)

325ml/11fl oz/1⅓ cups milk (at room temperature)
4 tbsp sunflower oil
2 eggs, lightly beaten
450g/1lb/3¼ cups gluten-free white bread flour
2 tbsp caster/superfine sugar
1 tsp salt
1 sachet (7g/¼oz) fast-action dried yeast/
    instant dry yeast

Pour the milk into a bowl, add the oil and eggs
and whisk together well to mix. Pour the mixture into
the bread pan. Sprinkle over the flour, covering the
liquid completely. Sprinkle the sugar evenly over
the flour, then add the salt. Make a small indent in
the centre of the flour and add the yeast.

Close the lid, set the machine to "Rapid Bake" (or
equivalent), then select the loaf size and crust type.
Press Start.

A couple of minutes after mixing has begun, lift
the lid of the machine briefly and scrape down the
sides of the pan with a plastic spatula to ensure
even mixing. Close the lid once again.

After baking, remove the bread pan from the
machine and turn the loaf out onto a wire rack to
cool. Serve in slices.

FRESH HERB BREAD

PREPARATION TIME 15 minutes

COOKING TIME varies according to bread machine

MAKES 1 loaf (serves 10–12)

400g/14oz/3 cups gluten-free white bread flour

55g/2oz/⅓ cup gram (chickpea) flour

275ml/9½fl oz/1 cup plus 2 tbsp water

2 eggs, beaten

4 tbsp olive oil

4 tbsp chopped fresh mixed herbs (such as parsley, basil, oregano and chives)

55g/2oz/⅓ cup freshly grated Parmesan cheese

1 tbsp caster/superfine sugar

1½ tsp salt

2½ tsp fast-action dried yeast/instant dry yeast

Combine the flours and set aside. Pour the water into a bowl, add the eggs, oil and chopped herbs and whisk together well to mix. Pour the mixture into the bread pan. Sprinkle over the cheese, then sprinkle over the mixed flours, covering the liquid and cheese completely. Sprinkle the sugar evenly over the flour, then add the salt. Make a small indent in the centre of the flour and add the yeast.

Close the lid, set the machine to "Rapid Bake" (or equivalent), then select the loaf size and crust type. Press Start.

A couple of minutes after mixing has begun, lift the lid of the machine briefly and scrape down the sides of the pan with a plastic spatula to ensure even mixing. Close the lid once again.

After baking, remove the bread pan from the machine and turn the loaf out onto a wire rack to cool. Serve in slices.

MIXED SEED LOAF

PREPARATION TIME 10 minutes

COOKING TIME varies according to bread machine

MAKES 1 loaf (serves 10–12)

325ml/11fl oz/1⅓ cups milk (at room temperature)

4 tbsp sunflower oil

2 eggs, lightly beaten

450g/1lb/3¼ cups gluten-free white bread flour

5 tbsp mixed seeds (such as sunflower, pumpkin, caraway, poppy seeds and linseeds/flaxseeds)

2 tbsp caster/superfine sugar

1 tsp salt

1 sachet (7g/¼oz) fast-action dried yeast/instant dry yeast

Pour the milk into a bowl, add the oil and eggs and whisk together well to mix. Pour the mixture into the bread pan. Sprinkle over the flour, covering the liquid completely. Sprinkle the mixed seeds evenly over the flour. Sprinkle over the sugar, then add the salt. Make a small indent in the centre of the flour and add the yeast.

Close the lid, set the machine to "Rapid Bake" (or equivalent), then select the loaf size and crust type. Press Start.

A couple of minutes after mixing has begun, lift the lid of the machine briefly and scrape down the sides of the pan with a plastic spatula to ensure even mixing. Close the lid once again.

After baking, remove the bread pan from the machine and turn the loaf out onto a wire rack to cool. Serve in slices.

ITALIAN TOMATO BREAD

PREPARATION TIME 15 minutes

COOKING TIME varies according to bread machine

MAKES 1 loaf (serves 10–12)

325ml/11fl oz/1⅓ cups milk (at room temperature)

2 tbsp oil from a jar of sun-dried tomatoes

2 tbsp olive oil

2 eggs, lightly beaten

55g/2oz/⅓ cup freshly grated Parmesan cheese

85g/3oz/¾ cup sun-dried tomatoes in oil (drained weight), patted dry and chopped

450g/1lb/3¼ cups gluten-free brown bread flour

2 tbsp caster/superfine sugar

1 tsp salt

1 sachet (7g/¼oz) fast-action dried yeast/ instant dry yeast

Pour the milk into a bowl, add the oils and eggs and whisk together well to mix. Pour the mixture into the bread pan. Sprinkle the cheese over the milk mixture, followed by the tomatoes. Sprinkle over the flour, covering the liquid, cheese and tomatoes completely. Sprinkle the sugar evenly over the flour, then add the salt. Make a small indent in the centre of the flour and add the yeast.

Close the lid, set the machine to "Rapid Bake" (or equivalent), then select the loaf size and crust type. Press Start.

A couple of minutes after mixing has begun, lift the lid of the machine briefly and scrape down the sides of the pan with a plastic spatula to ensure even mixing. Close the lid once again.

After baking, remove the bread pan from the machine and turn the loaf out onto a wire rack to cool. Serve in slices.

CHEESE & MUSTARD BREAD

PREPARATION TIME 15 minutes

COOKING TIME varies according to bread machine

MAKES 1 loaf (serves 10–12)

400g/14oz/3 cups gluten-free white bread flour

55g/2oz/⅓ cup gram (chickpea) flour

300ml/10½ fl oz/1¼ cups water

2 eggs, beaten

4 tbsp olive oil

3 tbsp gluten-free wholegrain mustard

85g/3oz /⅔ cup finely grated mature/sharp Cheddar cheese

1 tbsp caster/superfine sugar

1½ tsp salt

2½ tsp fast-action dried yeast/instant dry yeast

Combine the flours and set aside. Place the water in a bowl, add the eggs, oil and mustard and whisk together well to mix. Pour the mixture into the bread pan. Sprinkle over the cheese, then sprinkle over the mixed flours, covering the liquid and cheese completely. Sprinkle the sugar evenly over the flour, then add the salt. Make a small indent in the centre of the flour and add the yeast.

Close the lid, set the machine to "Rapid Bake" (or equivalent), then select the loaf size and crust type. Press Start.

A couple of minutes after mixing has begun, lift the lid of the machine briefly and scrape down the sides of the pan with a plastic spatula to ensure even mixing. Close the lid once again.

After baking, remove the bread pan from the machine and turn the loaf out onto a wire rack to cool. Serve in slices.

HERBED OLIVE BREAD

PREPARATION TIME 15 minutes

COOKING TIME varies according to bread machine

MAKES 1 loaf (serves 10–12)

325ml/11fl oz/1⅓ cups milk (at room temperature)

4 tbsp olive oil

2 eggs, lightly beaten

2 tsp dried Italian herb seasoning

85g/3oz/½ cup freshly grated Parmesan cheese

85g/3oz/½ cup pitted black olives (drained weight), chopped

450g/1lb/3¼ cups gluten-free brown bread flour

2 tbsp caster/superfine sugar

1 tsp salt

1 sachet (7g/¼ oz) fast-action dried yeast/ instant dry yeast

Pour the milk into a bowl, add the oil, eggs and dried herbs and whisk together well to mix. Pour the mixture into the bread pan. Sprinkle the cheese over the milk, followed by the olives. Sprinkle over the flour, covering the liquid, cheese and olives completely. Sprinkle the sugar evenly over the flour, then add the salt. Make a small indent in the centre of the flour and add the yeast.

Close the lid, set the machine to "Rapid Bake" (or equivalent), then select the loaf size and crust type. Press Start.

A couple of minutes after mixing has begun, lift the lid of the machine briefly and scrape down the sides of the pan with a plastic spatula to ensure even mixing. Close the lid once again.

After baking, remove the bread pan from the machine and turn the loaf out onto a wire rack to cool. Serve in slices.

SPICED HONEY LOAF

PREPARATION TIME 20 minutes

COOKING TIME 50–60 minutes

MAKES 1 loaf (serves 8)

115g/4oz/½ cup packed soft light
   brown sugar

85g/3oz/6 tbsp butter

175g/6oz/½ cup thick (set) honey

225g/8oz/1⅔ cups gluten-free plain/
   all-purpose white flour

a pinch of salt

1 tsp gluten-free baking powder

2 tsp ground mixed spice/apple pie spice

1 egg, beaten

150ml/5fl oz/⅔ cup milk

Remove the kneading blade from the bread pan. Remove the bread pan from the machine, grease and line the base and sides of the pan and set aside.

Place the sugar, butter and honey in a saucepan and heat gently until melted, stirring. Remove the pan from the heat and cool slightly. Sift the flour, salt, baking powder and spice into a bowl and make a well in the centre. Mix together the egg and milk and pour into the centre of the dry ingredients, along with the melted honey mixture. Beat together using a wooden spoon until smooth and thoroughly mixed. Pour the mixture into the bread pan.

Place the bread pan in position in the machine and close the lid. Set the machine to "Bake Only" for 50 minutes. Press Start.

After baking, a fine skewer inserted in the centre of the loaf should come out clean. If the loaf requires further baking, bake on the same setting for a further 5–10 minutes, or until cooked.

Remove the bread pan from the machine using oven gloves, then leave to stand for 5 minutes, before turning the loaf out onto a wire rack to cool. Serve warm or cold in slices.

VARIATIONS Use golden/light corn syrup in place of the honey. Use ground ginger or cinnamon in place of the mixed spice/apple pie spice.

STICKY SPICED TEABREAD

PREPARATION TIME 20 minutes, plus cooling

COOKING TIME 50–60 minutes

MAKES 1 loaf (serves 8)

115g/4oz/½ cup packed soft light
    brown sugar

85g/3oz/6 tbsp butter

115g/4oz/⅓ cup golden/light
    corn syrup

55g/2oz/2 ½ tbsp black treacle/molasses

225g/8oz/1⅔ cups gluten-free plain/
    all-purpose white flour

a pinch of salt

1 tsp gluten-free baking powder

2 tsp ground mixed spice/apple pie spice

1 tsp ground ginger

1 egg, beaten

150ml/5fl oz/⅔ cup milk

Remove the kneading blade from the bread pan. Remove the bread pan from the machine, grease and line the base and sides of the pan and set aside.

Place the sugar, butter, syrup and black treacle/molasses in a saucepan and heat gently until melted, stirring. Remove the pan from the heat and cool slightly.

Sift the flour, salt, baking powder and ground spices into a bowl and make a well in the centre. Mix together the egg and milk and pour into the centre of the dry ingredients, along with the melted syrup mixture. Beat together using a wooden spoon until smooth and thoroughly mixed. Pour the mixture into the bread pan.

Place the bread pan in position in the machine and close the lid. Set the machine to "Bake Only" for 50 minutes. Press Start.

After baking, a fine skewer inserted in the centre of the teabread should come out clean. If the teabread requires further baking, bake on the same setting for a further 5–10 minutes, or until cooked.

Remove the bread pan from the machine using oven gloves, then leave to stand for 5 minutes, before turning the teabread out onto a wire rack to cool. Serve warm or cold in slices.

VARIATION Use ground cinnamon in place of the ginger.

APRICOT & CRANBERRY TEABREAD

PREPARATION TIME 20 minutes

COOKING TIME 1–1¼ hours

MAKES 1 loaf (serves 10)

225g/8oz/1⅔ cups gluten-free plain/
all-purpose white flour

2 tsp gluten-free baking powder

115g/4oz/½ cup butter, diced

115g/4oz/½ cup packed soft light
brown sugar

finely grated zest of 1 small orange

175g/6oz/1 cup ready-to-eat dried apricots,
chopped

175g/6oz/1 cup sweetened dried cranberries

2 eggs, beaten

150ml/5fl oz/⅔ cup milk

Remove the kneading blade from the bread pan. Remove the bread pan from the machine, grease and line the base and sides of the pan and set aside.

Sift the flour and baking powder into a bowl, then lightly rub in the butter. Stir in the sugar, orange zest and dried fruit. Add the eggs and milk and mix together until thoroughly combined. Spoon the mixture into the bread pan and level the surface.

Place the bread pan in position in the machine and close the lid. Set the machine to "Bake Only" for 60 minutes. Press Start.

After baking, a fine skewer inserted in the centre of the teabread should come out clean. If the teabread requires further baking, bake on the same setting for a further 10–15 minutes, or until cooked.

Remove the bread pan from the machine using oven gloves, then leave to stand for 5 minutes, before turning the teabread out onto a wire rack to cool. Serve warm or cold in slices.

INDEX

ACKNOWLEDGEMENTS

My special thanks go to my husband, Robbie, for his continued support and encouragement with this book and for his tireless tasting of many of the recipes. My sincere thanks also go to Sarah Bradford and Bev Saunder for all their dedicated hard work testing recipes, and to Gwen Whiting for her help with typing recipes.